Patterns of Islam in Asia

by

Norman C. Rothman

ISBN: 1419648152

ISBN 13:   9781419648151

Library of Congress Control Number: 2006908011
CreateSpace Independent Publishing Platform
North Charleston, South Carolina

Contents

General Introduction

In Asia there are certain patterns in the practice of Islam which are the result of traditional culture, environment, historical patterns, and the mode in which Islam arrived. There patterns create conditions which result in syncretism and include other religions from the pre-Islamic period. Also influential is the role of Sufism in religion. Sufi brotherhoods helped form traditional Islam as opposed to fundamentalism. The final influence is general diversity reflected by various ethnic groups.

No single country has filtered Islam directly. Each country brings something from the past to the table, whether it is Hinduism in Bangladesh, animism in Indonesia, or Orthodox Christianity in Azerbaijan. In addition, pre-Islamic customs intermingle with Islam whether it is *adat* (customary laws) or nomadic practices and Turkic traditions. Third, in every Islamic country in Asia outside of the Middle East, the manner of Islam's arrival affected subsequent practices. In Asia outside of the Middle East, every country had Islam introduced partly or mainly through Sufism, the mystical devotional aspect of Islam. Sufism emphasizes individual meditation and communion with Allah. At the same time, conventional Islam is present through the Hanafi code of law. These currents of Islam tend to be relatively tolerant of other opinions.

The recent introduction of Wahhabi/Salafi currents into Asia beyond the Middle East (both of which stress fundamentalism) have injected a new element. Moreover, these new Islamists stress pan-Islamic politics, as exemplified by the Taliban in Afghanistan. The Islamic Movement of Uzbekistan (IMU) and Deobandi movement in Pakistan are currently challenging the status quo in their respective countries and neighboring countries.

There is considerable diversity in the Muslim community, as every city has both Sunni and Shia present. Although there are clashes between the two, with the partial exception of Pakistan recently, they have not yet reached the level of communal violence seen in the Middle East and Sub-Saharan Africa. In part this is due to certain commonalties for both Sunni and Shia. Both have been attracted to Sufism, and both belong to Sufi brotherhoods. These create bonds that often bridge sectarianism. It is these preexisting bonds that form a barrier to fundamentalism.

One must also consider the ethnic diversity within most Muslim-dominated Asian societies. Central Asia, for example, had and still has a large European component, specifically Russian, Ukrainian, and German minorities which date from the czarist and Soviet periods. Southeast Asia has large Chinese and Indian communities.

Also, each ethnic group has members outside their countries because of the way borders were drawn. Some countries have no defining group. There is no Afghan ethnic group, but there are different ethnic groups within the entity called Afghanistan. Pakistan is a similar invention.

The rise of literacy especially among youth, combined with the influence of globalism and the inability of the various economies to provide employment to match the skills of the newly educated, has provided a fertile ground for fundamentalism among youth. All of these factors will be dealt with through an examination of Islam as it exists in Indonesia and Malaysia in Southeast Asia; Afghanistan, Azerbaijan, Bangladesh, and Pakistan in South Asia; and Kazakhstan, Kyrgyzstan, Tajikistan, Turkmenistan, and Uzbekistan in Central Asia.

Introduction to Islam in Southeast Asia

Indonesia and Malaysia, which account for the majority of Muslims in Southeast Asia, have a number of similarities. First, their original culture and population majorities are Malay. As a consequence, Malay customs have commingled with Islam. Second, the type of Islam practiced in these countries reflects the way Islam arrived—through a combination of trade and war in Malaysia, and through trade, war, and gradual Sufi conversion in Indonesia. Third, a great deal of syncretism is practiced, as some influence from Buddhism and Hinduism, which predate Islam, continue to survive. Nonetheless, both countries view Islam as a source of identity, as they inhabit a territorial space not coterminous with historical boundaries. At the same time, Islam has been used as a form of differentiation between the Malay population and non-Malay minorities. As the populations are not totally homogenous, religious identity can be combined with ethnic identity.

Both countries have experienced rapid economic development that has affected other sectors of society such as education, urban development, political participation, and law, which offer a modern alternative to traditions, including Islamic prescriptions. The subsequent tension between modernizing tendencies and traditions, especially Islamic ones, has influenced the governments of both countries as they walk a narrow line between secularism and the role of traditional Islam. A compromise has been attempted between Islam as a dominant feature of culture and society and these modernizing tendencies. Despite verbal reinforcement, however, Islam is not the predominant feature in government. Nevertheless, with the increasing influence of external forces, the line between state and society appears increasingly narrow.

Islam as a Multifaceted Phenomenon in Culture: The Case of Indonesia

Introduction

Indonesia has received Islam over a long period from a variety of sources. During this period (over a millennium), it has intermingled with Buddhism, Hinduism, and indigenous animism in different parts of the archipelago in varying degrees. The result has been a complex picture of beliefs and practices.

This chapter will examine the different versions of Islam that currently exist in Indonesia. They can be termed traditional, modern, devotional, and syncretic. It r will examine each of these aspects as they have developed and currently coexist in Indonesia.

Background

Indonesia's geography, history, and politics have given the country a multifaceted blend of Islam. The country is the world's island chain. It is at the juncture of the Indian and Pacific Oceans as well as the South China Sea. It has a long history as an outlet for the huge Indian Ocean trading system that included East Africa, the Middle East, the Indian subcontinent, and Southeast and East Asia. Historically, pre-Islamic Buddhist and Hindu kingdoms based much of their economies (especially in Celebes, now Sulawesi, Java, and Sumatra) on their position as the eastern terminus of this vast trading system. The great land route (or land routes) collectively known as the Great Silk Road, which extended from China to Europe, also carried products from the Moluccas (now the Maluku Islands) and Bali, especially spices such as cinnamon, nutmeg, pepper, and cloves, which Europeans used as both flavoring and preservatives. In fact, the Moluccas were collectively known as the Spice Islands.

Although 203 million of Indonesia's 230 million people are Muslim (mostly Sunni, although there are Shia and Ahmadiya minorities), significant minorities such as Christians in the Moluccas and Hindus in Bali remain. Traditional animist beliefs are still common in parts of West Arian (Indonesian New Guinea), Borneo (Kalimantan), and Sulawesi. Islam arrived gradually. Missionaries reached Sumatra as early as 674 CE. Over the next thousand years, Islam spread gradually from Sumatra to Java to Celebes. Only in the last two centuries has it spread to Borneo,

New Guinea, and other island chains in the archipelago. Islam arrived from various sources — Mecca, Cairo, Persia, India, and China. After the arrival of the Dutch colonizers in the seventeenth century, Islam served as a nationalist rallying point, especially in Celebes, Java, and Sumatra. The cumulative effect of this disparate spread both chronologically and spatially has resulted in different traditions throughout the archipelago.

We will now describe the four chief traditions that currently exist in Indonesia. It should be noted that these are currents that interact with and are not discrete elements in the observance of Islam.[1]

The Sufi Tradition

Also known as devotional or mystical Islam, the Sufi tradition has been present in Indonesia since the beginning. Islam came to dominate much of Sumatra between the twelfth and fourteenth centuries, and much of Java between 1500 and 1700.

The center of Islam, then as now, was in the sultanate of Aceh in northwestern Sumatra. Acehnese scholars traveled constantly to Arabia and, upon return, were active in the foundation of Islamic brotherhoods, characteristic of Sufi beliefs.[2] Sufis are Muslims who seek personal knowledge of God. Often a Sufi withdraws from the world so as to concentrate on the remembrance of God and to follow the path toward knowledge of the divine.[3] Early Sufis followed an ascetic path by which the Prophet was looked on as the light of God. One sought to attain the destruction of all material desires in order to find a direct connection with the divine being. Asceticism led to ecstatic mystical experiences wherein one would commune with the divine, often through trances. The ultimate goal was for each personal heart to totally identify with God.[4]

To achieve this state, there is a seven-stage process. The first stage is repentance for past sins and errors. Subsequent stages involve include abstinence, renunciation, poverty, patience; trust in God, and acquiescence (satisfaction). During this process, the supplicant undergoes mortifications of the flesh. The initiate also seeks to attain a state of grace through experiences that center on love, hope, fear, contemplation, and meditation.

The Sufis have adopted a practice called *dhikr* that is based on the repetition of a formula that includes the name of God until the reciter falls into a trance. There are three stages. *Dhikr of the tongue* focuses on the verbal repetition of the name of G-d. The second, *dhikr of the heart*, stresses on the divinity of God within the heart. At this stage, the initiate is in or is supposed to be in the trance stage. The highest stage, *dhikr through one's actions,* represents the final stage wherein the suppliant attains the complete unification of self with God.[5]

The most prominent of Sufi characteristics was to form communities or brotherhoods in which they could practice their doctrines or practices in isolation. Each brotherhood would trace itself back to a founder as part of continuous spiritual chain. There are numerous Sufi brotherhoods, of which the two most prominent are the Quadiriyya and the Naqshbandiyya. The former is a global brotherhood, while the latter is identified with the Malay world.[6]

Other features are typical of Sufi observance in Indonesia as elsewhere in the Islamic world. Each separate Muslim brotherhood has distinctive approaches to dhikr. There are particular approaches as to physical posture, use of music, and breathing techniques. There is veneration of saints, or *walis*, attached to tombs in which wali remains are placed and attached near sites of brotherhoods. These tombs are the destinations for pilgrimages by adherents. Sufi "brotherhoods" are also open to women.[7]

Overall, Sufism has represented an alternative to the exclusive reliance to the Orthodox tradition that concentrated exclusively upon the Qur'an. Since the Qur'an was written in Arabic, and for many centuries prohibited from translation, Sufism that emphasizes the notion of many routes to God has enjoyed great popularity in non-Arabic-speaking Muslim countries such as Indonesia. Many people have embraced Sufism to such an extent that the terms *popular Sufism* and *folk Sufism* have emerged. In Indonesia, the following practices have been identified with popular Sufism:

1. Seeking protection from jinn (evil spirits) and the evil eye through the wearing of charms and amulets;
2. Using the Qur'an as a physical remedy for illness, such as drinking water in which a page of the Qur'an has been soaked;
3. Making pilgrimages to graves and tombs of saints;

4. Praying to deceased saints; and
5. Seeking *Baraka*, or blessings, by placing keys on the graves of saints.[8]

Syncretism

Islam came to Indonesia in Sufi form. As such, it gradually became synthesized with local customs. On Java, this syncretism came to be called, abangan. Abangan is an amalgam of indigenous beliefs with Hindu and Buddhist beliefs as well as with Islamic practices. Even within the orthodox observance of Islam, there is a separate current of thought called, kebatinan, which was a combination of animism, Hindu, Buddhism, and Islam. The latter was influenced by Sufism.[9] Kebatinan had become so established that it was recognized in the 1945 Indonesian constitution, and acknowledged as one of the official Indonesian religions in 1973. Suharto, who ruled Indonesia, from 1965 to 1998, openly followed this version of Islam.[10]

Kebatinan has a pantheistic strain as it encourages animal sacrifices and worship of both nature and ancestral spirits. These spirits are believed to inhabit natural objects, various objects and artifacts, and the graves of Muslim saints. If these spirits are not placated, illnesses and other personal misfortunes may result. To placate the angry deities residing in these spirits, pilgrimages and sacrifices are undertaken. If these fail, the services of a traditional healer are sought.[11]

One of the reasons that syncretistic practices remain popular is that Islam was originally practiced as an elite religion. Usually, it was only the elite who could read holy writs in Arabic. The continued popularity of abangan and kebatinan is the reaction of the masses in terms of accessibility to religion. Clifford Geertz, in his classic work, divides Muslims into three categories based on geography. His view is that the conversion to Islam was variable. Based on field work in Java, he believes that observance differed. Along the northern coast of Java, which was the first area to be penetrated by Muslims, pious observance dominates. These Muslims, whom Geertz terms *santri,* are rurally based and send their children to Islamic schools. Elsewhere, abangan is more common, as many peasants, although nominally Muslim, practice a variety of customs influenced by traditional beliefs. Members of the upper classes, although also nominally Muslim, put their religious emphasis on aspects of mysticism not only derived from Sufi beliefs but also from Buddhist-Hindu beliefs that preceded Islam. These observances and practices were termed collectively by Geertz as *priyaya*. In general, the type of syncretism practiced depends on the degree of penetration of Islam coupled with the dominant religious motif extant before the arrival of Islam.[12] Thus, Sumatra has the heaviest degree of pure Islam, while parts of Java and Sulawesi have strong admixtures of Hindi and Buddhist elements, and Kalimantan (Borneo) and Papua have strong animist elements. Adat, or customary Malay law, exists alongside Muslim laws or sharia in certain areas but is separate rather than syncretic.[13]

Modernist Islam

Since the end of the nineteenth century, a large segment of Indonesian Muslims have termed themselves modernists. They were influenced by the writings of Muslim theologians affiliated with the University at Al-Ahzar in Cairo who dealt with the challenges posed by Western colonialism to the world of Islam. Modernists advocated educational reforms within existing Muslim schools. Their objective was to strengthen the Muslim community by the introduction of new methods and new subjects.[14]

The modernists do not participate in Muslim brotherhoods and in general do not have much use for Islamic mystical rites. Overall, they do not put a high priority on ritual in their observance. Modernists put a greater emphasis on interpretation in arriving at decisions within the religious law. In general, they put much less stress on the teachings of great scholars, or *ulama,* from the past.[15] Their point of greatest deviance from the Muslim practices concerns the dead. Modernists do not follow ceremonies such as visits to saints and revered ancestors. They also do not engage in ceremonies that commemorate deceased religious teachers and their descendants. Most conspicuously, they do not participate in pilgrimages and visitations to the legendary Wali Songo, or Nine Saints (the eponymous founders of Islam in Java). All of these ceremonies are considered idolatry and thus sinful in the view of modernists.[16]

The modernist influence in contemporary Indonesia lies in two areas: its role in social organizations, and its role in supporting separation of church and state in post-independence Indonesia. Its primary social organization, the Muhammadiya, has branches throughout the country, and its members (over 30 million) constitute over 15 percent of the country's Islamic population. It was founded in 1912 and today runs numerous, clinics, orphanages, poorhouses, prayer houses, public schools, and universities.

In general, modernists support the teaching of secular topics, especially in urban schools.[17] This modernist support of a secular component as not directly antagonistic to Islam has carried over to support of separation of church and state. In 1945, in spite of pressure to make Indonesia an Islamic state, the founders argued that since large areas of the country were not Islamic, an insistence on Islam as a defining characteristic of the new state would lead to disunion. Accordingly, Indonesia was declared a "deconfessionalized" state, sharia was excluded from the federal legal code, and all persons were declared to have the right to worship according to their own religion. A ministry of religious affairs was established to deal with officially recognized religions such as Islam, Catholicism, Protestantism, Buddhism, Hinduism, and Confucianism. Attempts to make sharia obligatory for all Muslims have been successfully opposed by not only the Muhammadiyah but also its traditionist counterpart, the Nahdlayul Ulama (NU). The only state ideology since 1945 has been called *Pancasilla*, based on an acronym for nationalism, humanism, democracy, social welfare, and belief in God.[18]

Traditionalism

The abolition of the caliphate in 1923, the use of Islam in nationalist activities between the wars, and the reaction against the secularist orientation of the Constitution has led to a revival of traditionalism among Muslims. It has taken two forms: *pure traditionalism* and *revivalism*. Pure traditionalism arose in opposition to the modernist critique of Islamic learning. It looks on the past as a guide for the present. It observes many of the customs that the modernists criticize, such as visits to shrines, and emphasizes a strict interpretation of religious laws.

Nonetheless, this group advocates religious moderation and communal harmony. It joined (through the Nahdlayul Ulama) the opposition to transforming the constitution so as to make Indonesia an Islamic state. Nevertheless, there are clear differences. Observance is a part of a chain of transmission through generations to the time of the Prophet and even to the Prophet himself.[19]

The typical traditionalist organization is Nahdlayul Ulama (NU), which claims at least 40 million adherents, although some estimates have placed its membership as high as 42 percent of Indonesia's Muslim population. It was founded in 1926 and conducts the same type of activities as its modernist counterpart, the Muhammadiyah, with special emphasis on Islamic boarding schools, the majority of which it runs. The NU is the largest organization of its type in the country and, in fact, in the world.[20]

Although political parties based on Islam have not done especially well in elections since the fall of Suharto in 1998 (due in part to the split between orthodox believers known as *santri* on Java and the more blended Muslims of the abangan/kebatinan, and in part to the multiplicity of parties), traditionalists backed by NU have made progress in influencing the government toward Islam. In fact, the progress in the accommodation of Islam that has taken place over the past two decades may have reduced the incentive to vote for Islamic parties.[21] Another factor is the radical policies including violence and the intolerance of certain modern-day revivalist organizations (more on this a little later), which goes against the grain in relatively tolerant Indonesia and may have alienated voters against religiously based parties.

In any case, the moderation shown by traditional organizations has resulted in a series of laws and administrative actions that have served to accommodate Islam. In 1988, an education law made religious instruction mandatory at all levels of education at both public and private schools; in 1989, a religious court law was passed which strengthened the authority of Islamic sharia courts in such areas as marriage, divorce, inheritance, and endowment. In 1991 came the compilation of Islamic law for use in religious courts, the reversal of the law prohibiting head-covering (*jilbab*), and the centralization of agencies that supervise *zakat,* or religious alms. In 1992 there was the establishment of an Islamic bank, and 1993 witnessed the abolition of the national lottery.[22] There were other measures, including a bill to increase "piety" in education and Islamic cultural festivals, but the most significant acknowledgement of Islam came in 2001 when the central government granted special autonomy status to the restless Aceh region in Sumatra. As part of this autonomy, Aceh was granted the power to use sharia courts in matters affecting Muslims. The jurisdiction was, however, limited to civil matters. Enforcement would not depend upon public safety authorities but on societal consensus and public education (basically the suasion of public opinion).[23]

Attempts at Radicalism

Since the 1970s, one strain of Islam has been more assertive. Unlike more orthodox traditionalist groups, which deal with the present, these fundamentalist groups hearken back to an idealized Muslim Golden Age. They are truly fundamentalist in the sense that the Qur'an is the central point of reference and must be taken literally. These groups include Dakwah or Tarbiyah, a college student movement which has identified with the Muslim Brotherhood and the Hizbut Tahir, an Indonesian group which advocates a pan-Islamic caliphate. The Indonesian Mujahedeen Council, which advocates immediate implementation of sharia law in preparation for an Islamic state, and the Front Pembela Islam, which has a military brigade, are two additional radical groups. Another organization, the Ahl-al-Sunnah wa al-Jama'ah Forum, sent its military brigade, the Lasykar Jihad, to assist Muslims against Christians in Maluku (the Moluccas) and central Sulawesi (Celebes).[24] They have been so successful in their agitation that certain districts in both Sulawesi and Java are implementing certain aspects of Qur'anic scripture and sharia, like Islamic dress, the collection of *zakat*, time for performing prayers, and the allotment of more time for religious subjects to be taught in school.

Even though religion is not a regional responsibility, the desire to emulate Aceh in respect to Islamic jurisprudence is strong in these areas. The totality of votes of Islamic parties in elections has never been more than 37 percent, partly due to the reaction of the populace as a whole to violence and intolerance, even in a nation which is nearly 90 percent Muslim. Nevertheless, these groups and their political affiliates are very strong in certain regions.[25] Links to Al-Qaeda are evident in incidents such as the Bali bombing in 2002, which was linked to the radical Jam'ah Islamiya group, which seeks to unite all Muslims in Southeast Asia under one state. The aftermath of the bombing shows the inherent strength of traditional forms of Islam: the FPI froze its activities, and the Lasykar Jihad disbanded voluntarily. In general, most radical groups have eschewed violence.[26] Incidents such as these have tended to discredit radical groups in the eyes of many Muslims who support Islam, especially sharia in society, but not necessarily an Islamic state.

Conclusion: A Cultural Synthesis

Although most Indonesians are observant Muslims and pay obeisance to the role of Islam in society, they do not necessarily support the idea of an Islamic state. Traditionally, Indonesian society and culture have been absorptive to new ideas and have tended to absorb them in increments rather than as replacements. The four major traditions have tended to blend into each other. Thus, Sufis, syncretists, and traditionalists, for example, have all embraced the idea of worshipping saints. All four traditions respect both the Qur'an and the teachings of Mohammad. All four encourage both religious teaching and secular teaching, albeit in different degrees. Most except for the radical fringe support the separation of church and state. Nonetheless, Indonesia is a complex and changing society, and generalizations can change as societies do. Indonesia has always been receptive to currents from the outside world, and with new avenues of communication, global currents can sweep over Indonesia as they have done in the past.

The ongoing diversity and ubiquity of Islam as a result of the continuous presence of both global and local influences characteristic of the history of Islam in the country is evident in the prominent role of Islam in media and popular culture in today's Indonesia. The establishment of worldwide satellite communications, first through television and radio and then the Internet, has seen the flow of global influence which, unlike in some other Muslim countries, has not been blocked. The simultaneous flow of influence from without, as exemplified briefly in the atypical spurt of violence mentioned above in the early part of the 2000s that has now subsided, has actually reinforced the local tendencies of indigenous adaptations of Islam to blend together and permeate society as a whole to form the current cultural synthesis.

Mention has been made of the social work activities of both NU and the Muhammadiya. Both groups are engaged in similar activities in both social services and education where there is a vacuum to be filled. The latter area has been especially fruitful for both traditional and modern views of Islam to enter the culture. Indonesia never developed a high level of educational networks during the colonial period, so *pesantren* (traditional elementary/secondary schools) as well as Islamic universities have been established since independence. Both the pre-university and university institutions are often staffed by graduates of Western or westernized institutions rather than historic centers of Muslim learning such as Al-Ahzar in Egypt. Most of these institutions endeavor to combine a religious with a secular curriculum, in stark contrast to the Koranic schools and madrassas elsewhere, where learning is exclusively or predominately religious. Local syncretic and Sufi traditions are included, such as including Santri customs on Java, as previously mentioned, and the repeated recitation of God's name in religious instruction.[27]

Popular media reflects the combination of global and local influences, as is apparent in the ever-increasing media outlets which distill various Muslim and non-Muslim influences in an eclectic manner. The spread of literacy has led to newspaper columns and pamphlets written by popular preachers who disseminate their writings in snippets with a devotional subtext designed to inculcate some moral. In addition, as in other parts of the globe, the advent of electronic outlets such as radio, television, film, and audio-video cassette has increased the scope for popular preachers. In the past decade, the growth of the Internet and social media has brought a whole new younger audience for preachers.[28]

The age-old debate between traditionalism and modernism, in which the former emphasized the revelations as relayed through the Qur'an and the Haditha and the latter stressed the use of human reason and interpretation, has counterparts in popular print and electronic outlets wherein strict adherence to the Qur'an is coupled with the stress that each person should be in a position to apply the teachings of the Qur'an according to his/her own individual situation. It has become quite common for television programs, for example, to encourage strict adherence to religious ritual while simultaneously warning believers against doing anything they do not fully believe or understand.

Syncretism has continued to play a role in sermons and programs. These public outlets are continually laced with Arabic terms and the citations of Muslim authorities throughout the Muslim world, yet at the same time citation Western and non-Muslim sources whose beliefs may not coincide with the Qur'an and Haditha. Scholars routinely refer to the *umma,* the worldwide Muslim religious legal political community, yet simultaneously stress the Indonesian tradition.

The Sufi tradition continues to survive with the emphasis on the principle of *Istiqama*, or integrity or uprightness of faith. In many religious teachings in contemporary Indonesia, this principle is placed over the observance of often empty symbols. Istiqama will lead the practitioner to true holiness in the union with the reality of God. This concept is nearly identical with the Sufi ideal of communion with God. Combined with the stress on morning prayer, which brings the reciter closer to the creator in these teachings, the concept of dhikr, with repetition, leads to oneness with the Divinity.[29]

In general, religious programs and writings created a fusion between traditional and modern views of Islam that provided for applications to modern life. A religious principle would be invoked as a jumping-off place for the inculcation of a moral. A saying from the Qur'an or a teaching of the Prophet from the Haditha would be invoked to urge respect for elders, or the equal responsibility of both mothers and fathers to raise their children in the correct way. A subliminal message was that religious programs of various types often had females as hosts—electronic media propagating a traditional message applied to a modern situation with a nontraditional host! [30]

Indonesia has integrated Islam into its culture, and, in turn, been influenced by it. However, the country has received it on its own terms.

Modernity and Islam in Malaysia

Modernity

The concept of modernity dates from developments in Western Europe in the seventeenth century. At that time, the theological certainty of previous eras was challenged by a belief that causations could be multiple in nature, not just through divine intervention. It involved internal contradictions such as an emphasis on pluralism and stress on government centralization (ultimately leading to totalitarianism). There was an attempt to balance reason with faith as new attention was paid to the constructs of physical nature, human society, and history. The role of human experience in forging the environment and society was now examined. The previous emphasis on the providential and hierarchal Great Chain of Being broke down. Individual will and collective welfare arose. Hence, the conflict was often seen (until recently with the fundamentalist religious revival) not as much as a contest between the providentialists and humanists as between liberty and equality, or autonomy of local government and the centralization of state power (often under a charismatic leader). Both views placed their emphasis on the perfectibility of a civil society governed by human-made laws and rules, not an earthly society as a reflection of divine intention. Politically, this meant the elevation of the nation-state whose rulers would be selected through worldly means (usually but not always through election), not through divine intercession or secularism.[1]

Concomitant ideas found their way in all societal sectors. Economics, often seen as the embodiment of religious directives against interest or excessive interest and the theological ideal of the "just price," gave way to mercantilist ideas about wealth and power and capitalist ideas about the invisible hand of the free market among buyers and sellers, which would establish a market equilibrium. The Age of Science in the seventeenth century, the Enlightenment and rationalism in the eighteenth century, nationalist revolutions from the late eighteenth century, and the Industrial Revolution after 1750, along with the movement toward urbanization, mass education, and mass social and political mobilization after 1850, all advanced various aspects of modernity. The rise of mass technology in the past century, with its devices of both wired and wireless mass communication and the transfer of information via the Internet, have encouraged the development and homogenization of a universal global culture.[2]

It was perhaps inevitable that a Western paradigm that produced new bureaucratic and legal forms would provoke a reaction from communal, sectarian, and fundamentalist movements. Often, rather ironically, the forms of modernity—technology and mass communications in the guise of compact discs and the computer—have been used by resurgent traditional movements to oppose the substance of modernity, such as secular education and the separation of church and state. This opposition has been particularly striking with the resurgence of fundamentalist Islam that challenges the primacy of the nation-state in areas such as government and law, education, social structure, and economic development.

Islam has its own paradigm found in its various texts, especially the Qur'an. The Islamists have been selective about which aspects of modernity they oppose. They oppose pluralism, especially political pluralism, and the free will of the individual, especially in matters of faith. On the other hand, they support an all-controlling, even totalitarian central government, with the distinction that the all-encompassing inspired utopia is religious (Islamic) and the will of the people is the umma (community of believers).[3]

Background

Malaysia is the epitome of a nation and society that has attempted to balance aspects of modernity with an Islamic identity. Its present religious identity dates from the early fifteenth century (although present several centuries before) when a fugitive Indonesian prince converted to Islam, and converted the small settlement of Melaka into the most important trading state on the Strait of Malacca between the Indian and Pacific Oceans. He initiated the rise of Islam throughout the Malayan peninsula. Over time, Islam absorbed indigenous Malay beliefs.[4] Today, approximately 60 percent of the population of Malaysia, which also includes part of north Borneo, professes Islam. Although its constitution declares Malaysia to be a secular state, it simultaneously declares Islam to be the state religion. To add to this paradox, all ethnic Malays (about 60 percent of the population, although non-Malays who live in North Borneo are included in this figure) are officially defined as Muslim. The rest of the Malaysian population—Chinese, Indians, pre-Malay aboriginal peoples—practice a wide variety of religions. The Chinese practice Buddhism, Taoism, and folk beliefs; the Indians (of which there are a few Muslims) practice Hinduism and Christianity; aboriginals often practice animism. There are a number of Sikhs and followers of Baha'i. Unlike the Malays, the Chinese, Indians, and aboriginals are not defined by religion.[5]

Conflicting Visions

Because of the nature of the Malaysian polity—secular-oriented central government within a federal system that gives a large measure of authority to Islamic-dominated states within the existing federal structure, there is always a potential for conflict in the areas of law and government, education, and socioeconomic matters. The secular model in Malaysia professes that its goal is the well-being of its citizens, accomplished by existing federal law and especially the constitution. Thus, at the federal level, Malaysia implicitly pays lip service to the Locke/Montesquieu idea of a social contract/compact between the governors and the governed. The nation-state is the embodiment of a better life for all citizens in return for their allegiance. If it does not provide this better life, citizens can withdraw their allegiance (through elections or other means). Manmade laws and rules determine this process. In contrast, the Islamic vision posits a polity/ society comprised of all members of the legal/political/religious community, or *umma*. The umma is guided by the precepts of assorted religious writings such as the Haditha (Islamic sayings) and the Qur'an (the Muslim bible). The holy texts provide guidance for all facets of society. In the Islamic worldview, particularly the fundamentalist one, the government is judged by how well it carries out divine will, not man-made laws. If religious scholars, or *ulama*, decide that the government is not carrying out the dictates of Allah as revealed by holy writ, it can deem a government unjust and declare it illegitimate. The validity of the government is then challenged on this basis, not by consent of the governed.[6]

Government Practice

The constitution states that Malaysia is a secular state, but simultaneously declares Islam as the state religion. Although technically the country is not a theocratic state, according to a 1988 court ruling, there is no separation of church and state, as evidenced by recent prime ministers' declaration of Malaysia as an Islamic country. As defined by the constitution, one of the standards of Malay identity is the Muslim religion. A Malay would lose status if he or she renounced Islam. This means that the special privileges granted to Malays and other "original" peoples (termed *Bumiputra*) by Article 153 and government policies in term of affirmative action in university admission, government positions, special treatment in buying real estate and getting licenses, and general set-asides for business would be revoked. However, one does not become a Bumipitra by converting to Islam. This is a sore point because a number of Indians are Muslim, as are a small percentage of Chinese. Religion and ethnicity in regard to Malays in Malaysia are coterminous. Moreover, a recently developed identity card divides Malaysians into four classes based on religion: Muslims, Christian, Hindu, and Buddhist.[7] There is little doubt about the identity of the first category!

In actual policy, Malaysia has been dualistic in balancing modernity and Islam. At the federal level, developmental policies as embodied by the New Economic Plan have been handled by secular bureaucrats and were based on Western criteria. Countrywide policies, which concentrate on economic development and resource exploitation, have been the preserve of central government officials serving at the behest of modern elected political officials. However, nine of the thirteen federal states have constitutional monarchs or sultans. Although they ceded a number of powers to the federal government, they remained the supreme religious authority in their respective states. The country has two justice systems—a secular system based on laws passed by the elected parliament (the basic emblem of political modernity), and religious courts which administer sharia law. These courts are under the rule of the sultan and have authority over all Muslims. Even non-Muslims may fall under the jurisdiction of religious courts if a matter involves Islam, such as conversion. The states without sultans also fall under traditional religious rulers, as the chief of state is chosen every five years from among the hereditary sultans. These rulers have supreme religious authority.[8]

Law

As noted earlier, the country has a dual system of justice. At the federal level, laws are passed by parliament. Its judicial system is based upon English Common Law, which operates civil law based on the constitution. The court system includes the Federal Court, Court of Appeal, the High Court of Appeal, the High Court of Malaya (peninsular Malaysia), the High Court of Borneo (for East Malaysia in North Borneo), and a number of lower courts. The Federal Court, consisting of six judges, is the highest court of the land. It upholds constitutional matters, reviews decisions from the Court of Appeals, and settles disputes between states and between states and the federal government. Judges are appointed by the ruler upon the recommendation of the prime minister, as is the attorney general, the supreme legal official of the country.[9]

There is a parallel religion-based court system. The *sharia* system covers all aspects of Islam. This means it covers aspects of domestic law as well as estate law, involving the 60 percent of Malaysians characterized as Muslim. A non-Muslim affected by a decision made by a religious or sharia can appeal to a secular civil court under Article 121 of the constitution. However, in practice, these Islamic courts are often upheld. Recent court decisions have limited federal courts' jurisdiction over Muslim courts in matters that affect Islam. In addition, Muslim courts make room for pre-Islamic customary law ("adat") in deciding issues.[10] In effect, non-Muslims come under the secular civil law, while Muslim congregants often do not have this option. Recently, three women were whipped after being convicted of adultery; in 2011, another woman was sentenced to caning after conviction for drinking beer. These were decisions that were not appealed in spite of protests from the progressive women's movement, Sisters in Islam, that these actions were unconstitutional.[11]

Education

Education is the area where modernity appears most apparent, yet there is an undercurrent of tradition. The literacy rate now exceeds 90 percent and instruction is conducted in both Malay and English. Presently, Malaysia provides eleven years of free public schooling. As a result, over 99 percent of all six-year-olds are currently enrolled in primary schools (K–6), while nearly 95 percent of secondary school–aged children now attend secondary schools. The curriculum is quite familiar to anyone today. Primary schools teach basic skills such as reading, writing, mathematics, and basic science. Secondary education now offers academic and vocational tracks for career or university education. In addition, examinations are given at intervals in order to assess student progress. There are now a variety of colleges and universities, as well as postsecondary vocational and technical institutions.[12]

Since attendance at public schools is not compulsory, there are sectarian schools especially among the Chinese and Indians. These schools are permitted as long as they follow a nationwide curriculum. However, the Islamic resurgence of recent years has been especially prominent in education. Over the past twenty years, the objective (supported by the government) has been to infuse Islamic values wherever possible. Instruction in Islamic studies has been increased from 30 to 150 minutes per week. Islamic dress standards have been introduced. Moreover, teachers are now sent by the government to religious secondary schools. Several years ago, in line with the government Islamicization program, the state established an institutional Islamic university. Non-Muslim (basically non-Malay) students have some grievances, as Arabic script is now used in some schools. Also, they have to take a substitute moral education course and pass an examination in that subject. It has been obvious for some time that the Malaysian administration is moving toward a government-controlled, Islam-oriented educational system (signified as synonymous with Malay identity). Accordingly, Chinese and Indian schools lacking government support face a difficult future. It should be noted that homeschooling is allowed, which would favor sectarian/Islamic education, and one reason that vocational and technical programs have gotten support is to avoid a further polarization between Malays and non-Malays.[13]

Economic Development and Social/Political Mobilization

The nature of Malaysia's development over the past five decades has fed Islam-influenced efforts at mass mobilization in both the social and political spheres. The goal has been to reduce the discrepancy between Malays and non-Malays in business, the professions, and overall economic well-being. The disappointment of the former with the results has led to an increase in mass Islamic organizations and efforts by the government to accommodate Islam. After independence in 1957, there was an implicit bargain that the Malays would hold political power, while the Chinese would continue their domination in business. Nevertheless, Article 157 of the constitution indicated that the government would endeavor to uplift Malays through more training, business licenses, and support of rural development. After the Malay riots in May, 1969, the government embarked upon the new economic policy, which set up an affirmative action designed specifically to benefit Malays through state subsidies, scholarships, job quotas, and preferential licensing for various commercial, fishing, farming, and general commercial purposes. Companies were set up with the purpose of ensuring a minimum of 30 percent Malay ownership. Funding as well as tax concessions were made available to encourage companies to set up modern enterprises. Even after the emphasis shifted from top-down state directives to privatizations after 1990, large employers were encouraged to locate to cities by the inducement of cheap labor and the discouragement of labor unions. Malays whose rural holdings were too small to benefit from modernist assistance such as electrification were encouraged to move to urban areas to take these low-paying jobs. They lived in low-rent, low-quality areas. The country became more urbanized, and Malaysia showed high annual growth. But it was growth without development, as many Malays remained in poverty, and there was a widening gap between the haves and have-nots. Rural poverty now has been transferred to cities.[14]

Disillusioned by the gulf between the modernist elite and the continued poverty of the masses, many Malays turned to Islam, especially during hard times. Loss of employment without the traditional social network that existed in the rural areas created a vacuum into which Islamic associations stepped. Muslim mass organizations arose. Islamic ideals especially fit this set of circumstances. Islam has long preached the virtues of saving money and against the undue consumerism characteristic of the modern economy. It also favors zero-interest rates and an economic policy where buyers and sellers of both goods and services are treated equally through just prices.[15] This implicit criticism of materialistic consumption, the corruption money brought, and the accumulation of wealth characteristic of modern industrial society had a wide appeal.

Of more immediate appeal were the efforts of fundamentalist associations that became prominent after 1980. These movements, called *Dakwah*, have two aims. First is making Muslims better Muslims and converting non-Muslims; second is volunteerism through various economic, educational, and health endeavors. The first aim is represented by Jemant Tabligh, an organization active in rural areas and in urban centers as well as on university campuses. It emphasizes the use of Arabic in prayers as well as Arabic food and clothing. The second aim is represented by PERKIM, the acronym for the Islamic Welfare and Missionary Organization. This organization, along with other groups, provides for schools and adult education along religious lines. They also operate clinics along modern and Western lines. Perhaps most importantly, these groups manage and provide support for assorted small businesses. In times of economic downturn, these groups are vital lifelines providing income and employment.

There is a direct link between mobilized social and political organization. The Malaysia Islamic Youth Movement, or ABIM," the dominant university student movement, illustrated this connection. So powerful was this organization that its leader, Anwar Ibrahim, was taken into the government, where he rose to be the deputy prime minister until he was purged in 1999.[16] Nevertheless, since the time of his accession to the cabinet, the government, although not actively persecuting non-Muslims (with the exception of the controversial razing of Hindu temples and Christian churches), has increased the number of politically active Muslims in the bureaucracy, introduced some elements of sharia into the federal court system, and established an Islamic bank (as well as the university). The governing National Front Alliance, dominated by the United Malay National Organization (UMNO), has made these gestures because it is opposed by an alliance dominated by the Islamic Party of Malaysia (PAS) that makes electoral gains whenever Muslims feel that the ruling coalition is too secular.[17]

Conclusion

Malaysia walks a fine line in promoting modernity in order to foster development while paying obeisance to Islam. It must always be wary of Islamic feeling in terms of economic and social crisis. Therefore, the line between church and state remains ambiguous.

Islam in Southeast Asia: Concluding Statement

Both Indonesia and Malaysia have endeavored to introduce Islam into the modernizing aspects of law, economics, education, and politics while maintaining a secular emphasis in state and governmental matters. The impact of globalism, however, combined with mass communications and new prominence of Islamist forces, has tended to blur this line between society and state.

Patterns of Islam in Central Asia: Kazakhstan, Kyrgyzstan, Tajikistan, Turkmenistan, and Uzbekistan

Introduction

Certain common patterns are evident in the predominantly Muslim countries surveyed in this section. First of all, Sufism has played a major if occasionally overlooked role in the culture and practice of Islam in Asia beyond the Middle East. As a practical guide to individual study and through the prominent role played by Sufi brotherhoods, it has served as a bridge in various countries—a bridge between men and women, between Shia and Sunni, and between pre-Islamic culture and Islam. The brotherhoods perform many essential social services in these countries. Second, although fundamentalism has arrived in various guises throughout these Islamic countries, such as Wahhabism in Uzbekistan, and Salafism in Turkmenistan, individuals in these countries tend to follow the status quo Hanafi law code in these various states. Finally, each country has exhibited a certain amount of syncretism, whether it is traditional Turkic customs or preexisting aspects of Christianity and Buddhism before the arrival of Islam—all are intermingled with Islam to varying degrees in each country.

The Islamic countries covered in this study face similar problems. First, there are problems of identity. A number of these countries never existed until the past two decades. Nomadic societies such as Kazakhstan, Kyrgyzstan, and Turkmenistan never had centralized states within defined limits. A number of these countries, such as Tajikistan and Uzbekistan, have numbers equal or greater to their ethnic groups outside their borders as within these defined borders. This situation has led to strong irredentist feelings in these societies. In these cases, Islam has been used as a form of identity.

To one degree or another, these countries have been confronted by terrorism, whether homegrown as in Uzbekistan or imported such as Tajikistan or Kyrgyzstan. Fundamentalism has arrived in all of these countries but only in some has it transformed into violence. As a result, Islam has been a two-edged sword for the governments of these countries. On the one hand, they proclaim their modern nationhood through secularism. On the other hand, the profession of Islam has been a tool of this nationalism and a link to other more developed Islamic countries in the Middle East. The question then becomes the role of Islam in cohabitation with a nation state.

Other common problems which confront the countries under review revolve around economic pressures (such as economies not keeping up with the very high rate of literacy, which stems from the Soviet period), political corruption, and environmental problems (such as desertification in Central Asia). How do countries handle high unemployment for the young, as in Tajikistan for example? Is Islam useful in these cases, or does it become a focus of discontent? How do countries which now have high literacy rates and increasing populations of young educated people not fully employable in still developing economies meet rising expectations? Does this become an issue for fundamentalist Islam? How do the authoritarian regimes in countries such as Uzbekistan satisfy people who may be attracted to membership in an idealized pan-Islamic state?

Kazakhstan: Nomad Society into State

Central Asia has been a cultural transmission belt for two millennia. It has been a meeting ground of economic, political, and religious persuasions since Roman times. This aspect of Central Asia's position is best exemplified by the Great Silk Road. Actually a series of routes that traversed the ancient and medieval worlds between China and Europe, the Silk Road dominated global inland trade as well as empire building and religious diffusion. Islam reflects this interaction of various currents in the polarities that exist between Orthodox Sunni and Sufi beliefs, fundamentalist Salafi versus ecumenical Sufi orientations, and religious devotional feeling and secularism.

Kazakhstan composes two thirds of the central Asian landmass. It is over one million square miles, large enough to rank it the ninth largest country in the world by area. It is a country situated between various powers as it borders Russia, China, and three of the four other Central Asian countries—Kyrgyzstan, Uzbekistan, and Turkmenistan.[1]

The relatively sparse population of 16.5 million people is spread over a vast region of diverse ecologies, including deserts, dry steppes, and mountainous regions. The western region which borders the Caspian Sea is low and flat. The northern region consists of grass and plains comparable to the American northern Midwest. It is basically steppe country, with cold temperatures and snow 150 days a year. Nevertheless, it is fertile enough and warm enough to be the country's breadbasket. The central part of the country is semi-desert, while the southern part is mostly desert. This belt is similar to the American Southwest. Overall, the country has a combination of hills and mountains which are mostly in the east and often covered by forest.[2]

Diversity in Kazakhstan is reflected in its ethnic makeup. The entity of Kazakhstan as defined at independence in 1991 had inhabitants who tended to view themselves through ethnic and religious lenses rather than as common citizens. At that time, ethnic Russians who had migrated during the czarist and Soviet eras composed 30 percent of the population, while the indigenous Kazakhs made up 40 percent. The remainder of the population was made up of Central Asians, mostly Uzbeks, and nearly one million ethnic Germans, as well as several hundred thousand Ukrainians (both groups were resettled by Stalin during World War II). Russian had been the dominant language in Kazakhstan for over seventy years. The Russians were concentrated in northern Kazakhstan, and it was feared that the Russian population might secede. Although authorities feared secession, the Russians, as the largest seniority, were allowed to keep dual citizenship in both Russia and Kazakhstan. At the same time, they were not discouraged from migrating. As a result, over 1.5 million Russians left Kazakhstan during the 1990s. Most of the Germans also left, leaving only 350,000 Germans. Large numbers of Ukrainians also left.[3] At the same time, most of the predominantly Islamic Central Asians remained. In addition, the government encouraged hundreds of thousands of ethnic Kazakhs who lived in China, Mongolia, and Uzbekistan to return. As a consequence (combined with a relatively higher birth rate), there was a demographic shift, and Kazakhs were a clear majority by 2000.[4] It should be noted that although now ethnically less diverse, Kazakhs still tend to view themselves as members of three traditionally nomadic groups or hordes (called *zhuzes*, which will be discussed in more detail later) as much as Kazakhstanis.

Religious diversity was also present during this period. At least until the past decade, the Ukrainians as well as the Russians were Orthodox, and that religion, in addition to the German-influenced Protestantism, rivaled Islam. In fact, only in recent years has Islam enjoyed a majority of the population. Due to this heterogeneous background, religious observance has not been especially strict in the country. Even though most ethnic Kazakhs view themselves as Sunni Muslims, it is a very casual observance. Until recently the majority of Kazakhs professing to be Muslim did not really know some of the basic tenants of Islam.[5]

To understand the role of Islam in Kazakhstan one must view the history of both the country and Islam. Although an Arab army defeated the Chinese army at the battle of Talas near the southern border of Kazakhstan, Islam did not really penetrate the region to a significant degree until the eighteenth century (unlike much of the rest of Central Asia). Therefore, Islam did not take firm roots very early. The lack of a firm basis for Islam as a result of this history and the tribal structure of the country have persisted for centuries; particularly as a number of Kazakhs became Russified during the period of Russian domination between roughly the early part of the eighteenth century and until the end of the twentieth century.[6]

Kazakhstan's population has also been dominated by a clan and tribal structure which persists to this day. Historically the Kazakhs derive from parts of Genghis Khan's empire, specifically the Khanate of the Golden Horde. Although the Mongols had conquered a large section of the globe they were relatively few in number; so there was intermarriage with the Turkic speakers of Central Asia, also called Tatars. Ultimately, this led to the emergence of the Kazakh nation by the early fifteenth century.[7] Traditionally the Kazakhs have been divided into three confederations, or *zhuzes*—the Great Horde, Middle Horde, and Little Horde. The Great Horde, then as now, occupied the southern part of the country, while the Middle Horde occupied the center and the Little Horde occupied the west. (The north has been more diverse as the center for Russian and other European migrations).[8] These divisions have lasted till the present, and even though the hordes were officially abolished by the czar in 1848, the divisions remain. As independence approached, the zhuzes jockeyed for power. The Great Horde, in the person of Nazarbayev, whose wife was from a Middle Horde family, prevailed.[9]

Because of the nomadic nature of the populace, the role of Islam has been rather weak. There was only gradual access to Islam through missionaries who came to the south between 1200 and the 1600, but Islam was not really firmly in place until after 1800. As a result, Kazakhs have been open to a wide variety of influences. One example of this openness was the great influence of the Sufis, who appealed to the individualism of the Kazakhs. Sufism emphasizes a Muslim's direct personal relationship with God and stresses the spiritual aspects of Islam. It is less concerned with ritual and prescriptive.[10]

The other feature of Kazakh attitudes in regard to Islam is their relative tolerance of other religions. As Russia gradually expanded its influence into the Kazakh areas by the eighteenth century, Russians settlers brought their Orthodox religion with them. Other groups brought Catholicism and Protestantism. As the Kazakhs had an informal approach to Islam, they have been and remain tolerant of other religions. As discussed earlier, due to the extreme heterogeneity of the population (without a majority of Muslims until recently) and the parity between Muslims and followers of orthodoxy, this tolerance was really a necessity.[11]

The czarist rule between 1750 and 1918 followed by Soviet rule between 1918and 1990 witnessed various attempts at Russification.

As a reaction, many Kazakhs became actually more devout. In some ways Islam then became a badge of national identity for groups that did not have a strong sense of identity beyond the clan or ethnic group.[12]

Islam as a religion faced repression when the atheists and Communists took over during the Soviet period. Kazakhs practiced their religion secretly. The informal nature of Islam in Kazakhstan made it relatively easy to practice Islam in an informal and clandestine way. Religious classes and prayer gatherings were conducted in private homes, often in the evening. Madrassas and mosques were established as a way of commemorating religion, and often they were placed in out-of-the-way places such as remote valleys or even graveyards. In an unobtrusive fashion, Islamic scholars would often travel to low communities to perform religious rites. Officials turned a blind eye to these activities, as many of them were ethnic Kazakhs and thus sympathetic. In fact, quite often the Soviet functionaries were secret Muslims themselves. This conspiracy of silence was also an expression of nascent nationalism in a decentralized group. [13]

The years 1980–1991 were a transitional period as the Soviet Union gradually unraveled. Practicing Muslims began to openly express their faith. The number of mosques multiplied and operated openly. By the late '80s the opening of new mosques was almost a daily event in some parts of Kazakhstan. Even more significantly, Sufi shrines were restored or new ones were built. The shrines became the center of social and political activities.[14]

The role of Islam in Kazakhstan since independence in 1991 has gradually altered. Before the breakup of the Soviet Union, between 1979 and 1989, many young men from Muslim areas in the Soviet Union were drafted to serve in the Soviet campaign in Afghanistan. These men were influenced by the Afghan fighters against a secular government in favor of Islam. In addition to resisting fighting against fellow Muslims, a number of these conscripts were made aware of the fighters in Afghanistan who wanted to establish an Islamic state. Compared to other central Asian states, however, relatively few Kazakhs were recruited. The partial acceptance of these attitudes really occurred only in the extreme south, which borders Uzbekistan, the site of a number of extreme movements.[15]

Nonetheless, after independence in 1991, the government pursued a secular policy. It did partially support separation of church and states because of the polyethnic nature of Kazakhstan and the diverse religious situation at independence. The government also wanted to make sure it did not antagonize Europeans, who had many skills on which the country depended. The government also wanted to make sure the country did not get affected by extremism. The policy was in accord with the feelings of most Kazakhs. Because of this tradition, many Kazakhs felt that religion was a personal matter, and therefore a belief separate from the state.[16]

Since this time, however, with the opening of relations with other Muslim countries, especially those in the Middle East, Kazakhs have been allowed to travel, and study abroad has opened the country to other influences. Turkey, Saudi Arabia, and Iran have had contacts in the country. The development of oil industries has reinforced these contacts. As a consequence, many Kazakhs now feel that Islam should play a role in public life. In addition, the departure of Russians, Germans, and Ukrainians has reinforced the feeling for religion. There are also numbers of Chechens, Inguish, and Islamicized Koreans, as well as other Central Asians, and these groups all have made their influence felt. Overall, Muslims had reached 70 percent of the country's population by the 2009 census. Religious schools have also increased in the past two decades.[17]

In spite of these developments, the government has presided over the secular policy followed by its leader, Nursultan Nazarbayev, and has remained determined to be secular under his leadership. Kazakhs feel that they are a bridge between east and west and therefore do not have to be exclusively Islamic. Therefore, Kazakhstan is the only Central Asian country which does not give a special status to Islam. Instead, a separate religious authority has been established for Muslims.[18] Additionally, although the government has not prohibited the acceptance of financial contributions from Egypt, Turkey, and Saudi Arabia, it supervises these contributions and is careful to also supervise the construction and establishment of mosques and religious educational institutions. [19]

Successive Kazakhstan constitutions underlined the government commitment to separating religion from its public role in the country.

The 1993 constitution specifically prohibited religious political parties.[20] Further steps were taken in the 1995 constitution. This document specifically forbade any organization that sought to stimulate racial, political, or religious discord. It further imposed government supervision for all foreign organizations, including religious ones. [21] Because of terrorist activities related to Islam, the government has also taken steps to curtail foreign missionary work and has limited overseas study in Islamic countries. [22]

In general the Kazakhs have seen Islam as sign of ethnic identity rather than national identity and have used Islam for the latter. Most Kazakhs, however, continue to practice a folk version of Islam which includes beliefs and cultural practices that predate Islam. Except in the south, Islam was gradually introduced between the thirteenth and nineteenth centuries, and therefore a great deal of syncretism exists. As part of this tradition, the official head of Islam, or *mufti,* of Kazakhstan has supported separation of church and state as part of Kazakh tradition. [23]

Nevertheless, attendance at mosque is up dramatically, especially for Friday prayers. Participation in the *hajj,* or religious pilgrimage, has increased substantially. By 2010, the selling of *halal,* or purified meat for Muslims, had become quite common in many parts of the country, and the number of companies selling halal meat went from zero to five hundred. The wearing of the *hijab*, or head covering for women, has increased markedly. [24]

Overall, Kazakhstan is influenced in part by its tradition and by its adherence to the moderate Hanafi Sunni school so that it continues to be tolerant. This was exemplified by a bill passed on October 2, 2011 [25,] which simultaneously reemphasizes the role of Islam as well the Russian Orthodox Church but expressly protects religious freedoms and emphasizes religious tolerance.

Kazakhstan presents a picture of increasing penetration of a covered life by private organizations including Islamic, especially through education, in a country whose government as well as traditions are tolerant as well as secular. Only the future will show whether forces other than the traditional observance of Islam will produce conflict in Kazakhstan as it has in other countries in Central Asia that go back and forth between Islam and secularism.

Turkmenistan: Clan, Tribe, and Nation

Turkmenistan bases its new identity as a national state on two foundations: its Turkic identity and its profession of Islam. Until 1991, when it first gained independence, Turkmenistan had been a sort of turnstile, a gateway to Central Asia, located at the point between Central Asia, the Middle East, and South Asia. Turkmenistan borders the Caspian Sea (a body of water that is really an enormous inland salt lake). Turkmenistan's borders have been contested due to its internal situation as an area which until recently did not have a defined territory. It borders Uzbekistan and Kazakhstan to the north, Afghanistan to the east, and Iran to the south. Although it is the size of California, only 4 percent of Turkmenistan's land is arable. As a result, until the recent discovery of oil and gas, many people made their living through nomadic activities such as herding.[1] Turkmenistan's importance, then as now, was its location. Starting with the Persian Empire, which included Turkmenistan as part of its domain, Turkmenistan has always been a part of the states that have flourished. The Persians were succeeded by Alexander the Great, some of whose soldiers settled in the area. His successors formed the Seleucid Empire, which again included Turkmenistan. They were succeeded by the Parthians, a group related to Persians, who subjected most of Turkmenistan. They were replaced by the Sassanians, a Persian tribe. After the fall of the Sassanians through Muslim conquest, Turkmenistan came under Islamic rule. After this period in the eighth and ninth century, Turkmenistan was occupied by the Turkic group which now formed the basis of the emerging Turkic nation.[2]

Turkmenistan was very important because of its trading location along the southern reaches of the Great Silk Road. By the tenth century, its largest city at the time, Merv, which dated back to Parthian times, was an important textile center also known for its coinage, and had become an important center of Islamic learning. It was an important export center as part of the Great Silk Road.[3]

This importance coincided with the period in which the Turkic people coming in from 700 to 1000 converted to Islam. It was the Turkic influence which had and still has had the greatest impact on Turkmenistan. A branch of Turkic speakers, the Oghuz, had originated in the areas where Central Asia, Siberia, and Mongolia converge. They arrived by the ninth century. The period of 900 to 1200 was a time of glory. The Oghuz achieved the first Pan-Turkic Empire; when the Seljuk Turks (the Oghuz leader gave his name to this group of Turkic speakers) defeated the Byzantines in 1071 and went on to occupy Baghdad and much of Anatolia (today's Turkey). As Seljuk and his followers had come from Turkmenistan, the city of Merv was for some time the capital of the first pan-Turkic empire. It was this group whose zealous profession of Islam was a cause of the Crusades [4] For most of this area between roughly 900 and 1150, Merv was the largest city of this first Turkish empire. The city continued to be a center of the silk trade as well as a producer of cotton textiles, and a number of routes still converged in this area. Control of Turkmenistan was therefore very important due to its strategic location.[5]

The golden period declined after 1150–1200 due to a series of invasions, particularly by the Mongols in the 1220s. By 1400, Turkmenistan had become relatively nomadic, divided among the tribal groups and clans. This situation continues today in terms of tribal and clan organization. After 1400, it had ceased to be a political center and was the object of struggles between the Persians in the south and Uzbek Muslim khanates to the north. These khanates, such as Bukhara and Khiva, struggled between themselves and with the Persians to control the country until the Russians took over in 1885.[6]

Islam and Turkic influences arrived at about the same time and have comingled ever since. Of all the Central Asian states, Turkmenistan continues to practice and follow traditional beliefs the most. Turkmen have combined private life and customs with public adherence to Islam. Traditional beliefs include seventeen separate deities and are combined with Islamic teaching. The most common example of this combination or syncretism was the identification of the most powerful of the traditional deities, Tengri (Eternal Sky), with Allah.[7]

Islam in Turkmenistan has tended to be informal. Although Arab and Persian influence were instrumental in a military sense, Islam in many cases arrived by a peaceful means to traders along the Great Silk Road and through the missionary activities of the Sufis. The mystical teachings of the Sufis have stressed personal communion with God over ritual and dogma. This approach has resonated with Turkmen. Therefore Turkmen find it easy to incorporate traditional beliefs with Islam. Sufi use of various dances, music, and other folkloric elements has appealed to the great majority of people who practiced these customs in pre-Islamic times. Sufis often encouraged the Turkic tribes to continue their traditions while practicing Sufism, and the local Sufi leader often became identified with the traditionalists' religious leader and become a tribe or clan's religious guide, to be worshiped as a saint, a common feature of Sufism. Again, this was a way of adapting to previous customs.[8]

Sufism exerted influence also through Sufi preachers and religious brotherhoods. As a consequence, during Soviet times, atheism did not really penetrate Turkmenistan. *Adat*, or traditional customs, tend to be the dominant element in religion, and people follow the rules and customs of their Turkmen ancestors. Turkmen custom was so predominant a common saying goes, "You can renounce religion, but customs never," (see note 21). The practice of following the rules of their mythical ancestor, Turkmenchilik, is still prevalent. Turkic society continues to be based on neighbor, community, clan, and tribe, with elders playing a prominent civil as well as religious role. This role combines with magic, tribal superstitions, and aspects of shamanism and witchcraft. Because strict Muslim customs never played a role in how religion was practiced in Turkish culture, attempts to suppress Islam by first czarist and then Soviet regimes did not really affect Turkmen. It was certainly a cause, though, of the outbreak of rebellion along with other Central Asian territories in 1916 during the Basmachi rebellion in 1916–1920, which was caused as much by conscription and Russian soldiers as by religious repression.[9]

Under the Soviets, the mosques were closed, as were Islamic schools, and the teaching of Islam was prohibited. However, as Islam could be practiced in a traditional way in Turkmenistan as part of their customs, these prohibitions meant very little in practice for Turkmen. Individualistic in their practice, Turkmen observed Islam in homes, fields, and even on sidewalks. Therefore, the closing of formal Muslim institutions and prohibition of orthodox observance in terms of Islam were meaningless. In general, Islam for Turkmenistan today is really a cultural experience rather than a religious one. Islamic customs are observed on formal occasions such as weddings, funerals, and baptisms.[10]

This approach to religion has continued until the present. Since independence, the government, under Sapamurat Niyazov and his successors (since 2006, his son) [11] is very mindful of the political aspects of

Islam and its effects in neighboring countries such as Iran, Afghanistan, and Tajikistan. Consequently, it has to the present tried to prevent the same situation from happening. Accordingly, the government controls Islamic institutions through a Council of Religious Affairs. It pays Muslim clerics directly, and governments have to issue permits to build mosques. Government permits are required to hold religious demonstrations and meetings. In addition, the constitution established freedom of religion. There is no specific mention of Islam as the official religion; indeed, there is no mention of any religion as the state religion.[12]

The government does, however, differentiate between its support of separation of church and state and its support of Islam as a badge of national identity along with Turkmen traditions. This distinction is important in a country which really never existed as a separate entity until 1991. Accordingly, Islam has an important role in reinforcing both ethnic and national identity. To this end, public schools in Turkmenistan are instructed to teach Islamic principles within their curriculum. The government has also built religious schools to train new clerics, and has used public funds to build new mosques and repair old ones. As literacy is now almost 100 percent as in most other former Soviet states, this educational requirement is an important consideration.[13]. The government has also solicited funds from other wealthy Islamic countries such as Saudi Arabia and the Gulf states to support these endeavors.[14]

If there were a contest between Turkmen traditions and Islamic customs, the former would win out. Although Islamic for over a millennium, Turkmen society has always accorded women much more freedom than do many other Muslim societies. As an example, women have never been forced to wear veils or be segregated from men. These practices exist due to a nomadic tradition wherein women are often treated equal to men in terms of the economic situation.[15] During the Soviet period, many women entered the work force and were trained to perform professional positions. Women received equal education to men. Unlike many other Islamic countries, the Republic of Turkmenistan, in its 1992 constitution, specifically stated that men and women have equal rights. Women have equal rights in inheritance and marriage, which also puts Turkmenistan at the forefront in this area among Muslim countries.[16]

Literature and the arts have always been more Turkic than Islamic, as in oral poetry, which has been recorded in the Turkmen language and read in Turkish script even by Sufis. Education is free and compulsory until the eighth grade and is in Turkic. Latin/Roman script has been introduced for school subjects and Turkmen now take English as a second language in K–12 and at the university. Religious schools are not permitted. Religion may be encouraged at the private level but may not interfere with state-building goals, which emphasize national identity and Turkmen individualities. Overall, Turkmen put their culture first and Islam second.[17]

In general, spiritual activities revolve around the cult of ancestor worship in Turkmen tradition especially the descent from the four holy tribes. In many ways, Islam in Turkmenistan departs from the norm. Turkmen look at Islam as part of a national culture, which may include both secular or non-Islamic elements as well as Islam. Folk Islam is always predominant over orthodox Islam. Turkmen are concerned with life events and other practices such as sacrifices and mysticism along with Sufism, which has acted as a barrier to political Islam and the rule of sharia. Traditional Turkmen customs and Sufi practices that emphasize pilgrimage to shrines, use of magic charms, and the presence of divinity in plants as a tool against evil eye are quite prominent in Turkmenistan.[18] This traditional emphasis is hardly orthodox Islam.

Overall, the nature of Turkmen society has acted as a barrier to formal orthodox Islam. People prefer to worship in private, even when a mosque is available. Professional clerics have never been prominent. Sufi teachers are more influential than the *ulama*, or religious scholars. Islamic judges are not present. [19]

For Turkmen, customary law, adat, supersedes Islamic law. Mosques are usually empty except for Friday prayers. This virtual nonattendance usually occurs even in Central Asia's largest mosque, the Turkmenbashi Ruhe; built in the hometown of President Niyasov.[20] The government has taken various steps to curtail political Islam beyond statements in the constitution. In 1994 the Gengish (the council of religious affairs) received the right to control the selection, promotion, and if necessary the dismissal of clergy.[21] In 1999, many of the new mosques were closed. Earlier, the government had closed all specifically Islamic institutions. Foreign religious literature was banned, and education at madrassas abroad has been limited. Pilgrimages to Islamic holy places and Mecca are also limited to 188 people, well below the quota established by Saudi authorities—really about 5 percent of the total. [22]

Aware of the role that Sufism has played as a barrier to political Islam, coupled with the emphasis on Islam as part of national culture, the government has basically reinforced the tradition of Sufism through its encouragement the pilgrimages to the graves of Sufi scholars. Moreover, the sayings of the president, the Rukhnama, were published as a book and required to be displayed inside mosques as well as in various schools. Nizasov's book, at least during his lifetime, was placed on a par with the Koran. [23]

This combination of Sufism, tribal customs, traditional nomadic Turkic belief systems, and government policies has given Islam an informal position rather than a public role. This situation may change in the future, but it does not seem imminent at this time.

Tajikistan: Iranian Outpost in Central Asia

Tajikistan has had a recent turbulent relationship with Islam. In some ways, Tajikistan differs from its neighbors. It is part of the Iranian culture which preceded the Turkish cultural belt as a dominant complex in Central Asia. As a consequence, its language is not Turkic but is related to Persian. This results from the influence of the Persian Empire in the fourth century BCE.[1] As in other parts of Central Asia, Islam was initially introduced by Arab military conquerors in the eighth century. Historically, like other countries in Central Asia, Tajikistan has been fairly open to other ideas and is similar to other Central Asian countries in that Islam is as much part of the country's cultural heritage as it is its religion. Unlike its Iranian cousins but like most of other Central Asian countries, most people are Sunni. This is an important difference in the contest for influence among Iran, Saudi Arabia, and Turkey. Topography has conspired to divide Tajikistan into northern and southern lowlands where most Tajiks live. These densely populated areas are separated by mountain ranges, especially the Pamirs, which are among the highest in the world and are comparable to Tibet and Nepal in elevation. This topography has conspired to make a unitary government for Tajikistan very difficult.[2]

Second, in Tajikistan the people lack the tribal nomadic Turkic tradition which has acted as a binding element in other Central Asian states. Third, the Sufi heritage is strong in Tajikistan as in other Central Asian countries, and it is especially prominent in the southern part, though not as strong as elsewhere in Central Asia. However, the Islamic fundamentalist influence has been much stronger in Tajikistan than in other Central Asian countries, particularly in those areas which were not ethnically Tajik such as Badakhsan, which is inhabited by the minority Pamir group. The relative strength of Orthodox Islam in the country was shown in 1916–1920 by its strong support of the Islamic revolt in Central Asia that has been noted in other chapters. In fact, this revolt began in Tajikistan. Islam required a strong identification of people in the isolated mountains and valleys, but Islam tended also to be filtered through Sufi leadership who basically brought a more secular influence through this filter and came to dominate some part of Tajikistan's culture and ethnic self-awareness.[3]

Regionalism has played a part in post-independence Tajikistan. The Soviet nomenklatura, which was based in the north of the country, inherited power. The other regions were traditionally resistant to Soviet authority; however, and in 1916–1920 were the center of religious revolt which in some places lingered until the 1930s. Two regions were especially resistant: the Karategin Valley and Badakhashan. They tended to turn to alternate noncommunist ideology, including strong adherence to Islam.[4]

This was not the same fundamentalism represented by the Iranian Shia or Saudi Wahhabis but rather was dominated before 2000 by organizations that were somewhat indigenous. During the last decade, however, characteristics of Islamic fundamentalism have begun to change for several reasons. First, Tajikistan, as was the case for many Central Asian states, has achieved through the Soviet era near universal literacy. In addition, Tajikistan has the highest birth rate in Central Asia and thus has been unable to employ the educated youth who graduated from secondary schools and universities. Moreover, the country in some ways is the poorest in Central Asia, so that about 60 percent of Tajiks often look for jobs outside of the country.[5] A great many Tajiks have immigrated to expatriate areas; the largest number of Tajiks lives in Afghanistan where they are one quarter of the population (the second-largest group). There are also significant numbers of Tajiks in Uzbekistan. The struggle against the Soviets and then against the Taliban involved Tajiks who often led resistance to first the Soviet regime (after 1979), and then young Tajiks who were radicalized by the Taliban.[6]

Another cause of difference between Tajikistan and other Central Asian countries was the five-year war that broke out in Tajikistan in the 1990s and involved the Islamic-dominant coalition against a government that was comprised of former Communists. Conflict led to over fifty thousand deaths, and another 10 percent of the population of the country left the country.[7] The end of the war gave opposition figures, including Islamic ones, a role in government, but they have gradually been forced out, or ultimately imprisoned or liquidated. This action has hardened Islamic opposition to the government in recent years. A number of Tajik Islamists have embraced the concept of an ideal society ruled by sharia and have viewed Tajikistan as part of the worldwide Islamic state or caliphate. These beliefs have not yet reached the masses but are gaining momentum in a society that has previously been noted also for folk Islam and toleration to other faiths such as Orthodox Christianity, Nestorianism, and the Persian-based faith of Zoroastrianism.[8]

A drift toward radicalism is exemplified by organizations originating from countries such as Pakistan and Saudi Arabia. (A more benign manifestation is the construction of new mosques). Originally, these countries recruited Muslims to fight against the Communists in Afghanistan. Two sects, the Deobandi, a sect founded in north India in the nineteenth century and now centered in today's Pakistan, and the Wahhabi, which originated in Saudi Arabia in the eighteenth century, have been active, and they have basically encouraged both anti-Shia and anti-Sufi sentiment. In addition, they have taken a negative view of worship at shrines and the position that opposed the improvement of women's status. The center for these organizations was in the Ferghana Valley, the most fertile area in Central Asia, which is split among Tajikistan, Uzbekistan, and Kyrgyzstan. The end of the restrictive policies of the Soviet Union led to revival of outward observance of Islam that resulted in the building of mosques and Sufi shrines. [9]

The Islamic Renaissance Party became the chief component of the opposition to government in the early 1990s and was the only recognized Islamic-based party in Central Asia. It was a center of Islamism in Central Asia. The civil war that took place in 1992 was led in part by the IRP and also consisted of support from the Sufis and their brotherhoods. Originally, a number of Tajik nationalists supported them even though the party was founded by Islamists in Russia and Tajiks abroad. In the first election in 1991, the IRP received over 31 percent of the vote.[10] However, the failure of the Tajik-dominated government in Kabul persuaded the IRP to enter the government of Tajikistan proper. It was divided into factions, one that claimed that Islam should be citizens' private business and the other which maintained that Islam should play a state role. This split among the factions as well, as the clan-based and topographical nature of Tajikistan and subsequent regionalism, led to in-fighting. The lack of economic progress in spite of American aid specifically after 9/11 (when the government made arrangements with the United States for defense, including a military base), combined with increasingly harsh measures against Islamism, ultimately led to the decline of the IRP.[11] As a result, the party came a distant third in elections in 2000, receiving only 8 percent of the vote (after having entered the government in 1997 following the civil war). In recent years, government has not outlawed political parties based on religion, but it routinely cracks down on what it terms "Islamic extremists."[12]

The parlous economic situation of underemployment or no employment has aggravated the situation in Tajikistan, and the country is estimated to have underemployment of 40 percent.[13] The result has been that some of the IRP membership have migrated to more radical associations such as the Hizb-ut-Tehrir or HT organization as it is sometimes called. This underground movement, which also has branches in Uzbekistan and Kyrgyzstan, promotes the unity of all members of the Islamic legal political community, or *umma*. It believes that all Muslims should be under a universal state or caliphate and in the implementation of sharia. Even though it sees jihad as a tool, it advocates bringing change in a nonviolent way. If this change is achieved, it maintains societal problems will be solved. It is, however, in spite of its emphasis on nonviolent change, intolerant of other religions and other forms of Islam. It is located in the strategic Ferghana Valley and, because of this, making it is an influential organization.[14]

A more violent organization is next door—the Islamic Movement of Uzbekistan, which has gradually changed its name to the Islamic Movement of Turkistan—and has also encouraged Islamic fundamentalism. Unlike the HT, the IMU advocates violence to establish an Islamic state under sharia law as part of the universal caliphate comprised of umma members. Because of the relative weakness of the central government of Tajikistan, this movement often has used Tajikistan has a springboard for raids into Uzbekistan.[15]

Although the Tajik government has cracked down (within its capabilities) on the fundamentalist movement, it does not want to rock the boat. The minority groups such as the Pamiris, who espouse the Ismaili sect, an offshoot of Shia, are tolerated. Since the population is over 90 percent Muslim, the government has recognized Sunni Islam of the Hanafi school as the official religion of Tajikistan, although as discussed previously, it tolerates other groups.[16] Demographics have dictated this decision. A high fertility rate among Tajiks and migrations of Russians and other Europeans has strengthened the Muslim element.[17]

Overall, in spite of its recognition of the increasing Muslim character of Tajikistan, which is now over 90 percent Muslim, and indicating

Islam as a state religion, the government of President Rahmonov remains determinedly secular. In fact, a law was passed banning youth under eighteen from attending mosques in groups. At the same time it also banned girls from wearing jewelry except earrings, and prohibited youth under twenty from getting tattoos as well as watching films or reading books on extremism and terrorism. In general, the government does try to appeal to conservative feeling while opposing extremism.[18]

Previously students from religious schools abroad were called home. The government has imposed sermons on imams to deliver at mosque related to fighting against radicalism. Recently it went further and dictated that fifty-two of these sermons, or one a week, be delivered at mosques each year. In 2011, men with beards were arrested and made to shave.[19]

Tajikistan survives on remittances from abroad as many young men work outside the country, including in Muslim countries. The government fears that these young men are being radicalized, but it has no alternative given the extreme poverty of the country.

Although the majority of citizens continue to practice the informal customary religion rather than formal Islam, the economic circumstances are providing a fertile recruiting ground for extremism. Young men desperate for work in a very poor country will increasingly be attracted to alternate philosophies that promise solutions to worldly problems.[20]

Uzbekistan: the Keystone of Central Asia

Uzbekistan is the key country geographically in Central Asia as it borders the other four countries. It is the largest state in Central Asia, with a population of over 28 million (about half of the region's population). The Uzbek people (not all people in Uzbekistan are ethnic Uzbeks) account for large percentages in other countries as well—close to 25 percent in Tajikistan and in Kyrgyzstan, and a significant percentage in Kazakhstan, Turkmenistan, and Afghanistan.[1]

As was the case in Turkmenistan and Kyrgyzstan, Uzbekistan was an important stop on the Great Silk Road. By 1500, the Uzbeks had established themselves as the main Turkic-speaking group in Central Asia. Its independent khanates of Bukhara, Kokhand, Khiva, and Samarkand were the centers of both wealth and learning. The cities of Bukhara, Samarkand, and Tashkent were celebrated for their wealth and Islamic learning. As has been the case in the other Central Asian states, the Russians took over the khanates in the nineteenth century and the Soviets by 1920.[2]

As in other Central Asian states, Islamic practice centered on indigenous customs and went underground during Soviet period. Although Uzbekistan shares in the Sufi tradition and Turkic folk tradition, it also had a larger formal Islamic structure because of its centrality in Turkestan (the former name for Central Asia) and the prominence of its urban centers over many centuries. Samarkand in particular was important even before the arrival of the Uzbek people around 1500, as it was noted for its Muslim scholars.[3]

Faced with the usual repression of religion during Soviet times, the people of Uzbekistan engaged in Islamic observance through the attending of secret mosques and the spreading *samizdat* (underground literature) on religious matters and various other formats. The last two decades have seen the arrival of traditional Islam as exhibited by the construction of thousands of new mosques and hundreds of new madrassas, but with professions of Islam expressed mostly in traditional Uzbek customs in life cycle ceremonies as most Central Asian countries did during the Soviet period and after.[4] The country has declared itself in favor of separation of church and state and there is no official religion. As major cities often have a large dominant Tajik element, especially Bukhara and Samarkand (Tajiks may account for almost 25 percent of Uzbekistan's population), the government worked to strengthen the Uzbek element, with an emphasis on the national element through language and related cultural institutions such as religion, in an attempt to nationalize a population that was up to 40 percent non-Uzbek, including Russian and other Central Asians.[5] As a relatively cosmopolitan country because of its cultural heritage, Uzbekistan includes virtually every Muslim group from the former Soviet Union such as the Uighurs, assorted groups of Turks, and Muslims from the Caucasus who were deported by Stalin during WWII, as well as non-Muslims such as Armenians, Russians, and Jews. Religiously, however, due to a migration of non-Uzbeks and non-Muslims, 90 percent Uzbek people profess Islam. Furthermore, a large number of Tajiks speak Uzbek, so basically the country has become more homogenous.[6.]

As the leading Central Asian country, in the last two decades, Uzbekistan has tried to balance its agriculture, mostly cotton cultivation, commerce, and mineral production, especially gold, oil, and gas. Nevertheless, as in most other Central Asian countries, the economic situation is not good and large numbers of people have to work outside the country to have employment.[7]

The combination of economic difficulties and the harsh rule of Islam Karimov, a former Communist who took over the leadership at independence, have led to a reaction during post-Soviet period. This reaction has assumed the form of fundamentalist Islam during last two decades. One example is the Hizb-ut-Tahir, or HT or Party of Liberation, which, as discussed in the chapter on Tajikistan, favors a universal Islamic state under sharia law. It is active in Uzbekistan, Tajikistan, and Kyrgyzstan and maintains that it is nonviolent. Another example is the Nursi movement, the followers of the leader of a Turkish revival movement. This movement began in Turkey and attempts to tie religion to science. It is active in media and the education. Finally, the most radical and violent movement is the Islamic Movement of Uzbekistan. It has spilled over into neighboring countries such as Tajikistan and Kyrgyzstan. It is in fact an armed movement and has for a number of years and under various names been the main purveyor of terroristic attacks both inside and outside Uzbekistan.[8]

The key event in recent years that has added to extremist feelings (although the bulk of Uzbeks continue to practice informal folk of Islam and don't support pure Islamic fundamentalism except in reaction to economic and political causes), was the Andijan Massacre, in which hundreds and perhaps thousands of protestors were shot (although the official count is 187) when they protested for economic reasons. The assistance of the United States, which has had a military base since 2002 in the aftermath of 9/11, and later assistance from both China and Russia have not truly improved the situation. The government has responded to all fundamentalist and non-opposition by labeling it terrorism and reacting often in violent ways.[9]

Some of the largest opposition groups to the present regime have a religious orientation. The previously mentioned HT or Party of Liberation was founded by Muslims in Russia in 1953 and has members worldwide including in Europe and America. As mentioned in the Tajikistan chapter, the party seeks a universal state under sharia law. Although recently it has claimed to be tolerant of other religions, it remains suspect, as it rejects freedom of religion and equality of women. It has been active in prison ministries that may be used for member recruitment. Even though it continues to claim to be nonviolent, and says it wants people to come naturally to the organization, it is looked upon with disfavor by the government. Most of its members in Central Asia and in the former Soviet Union, now Russia, are ethnic Uzbeks. Although not officially outlawed, its members are harassed, monitored, and subject to what it considers unfair persecution.[10]

The Nursi movement, as indicated earlier, is the Turkish Islamic revival movement which attempts to bring religion and science together. It argues that the Qur'an helps all readers to the revealed truth by use of reason and reading the texts by reason as well as by faith. This revelation of the truth can be found in the text of the Qur'an and other basic Islamic readings. Reading the Qur'an and other readings and using logic makes the reader realize that there is only one explanation for the universe, which the holy texts explain, as they explain everything in the universe. These writings from the founder of the movement have found favor among intellectuals in Uzbekistan since they offer a different attitude toward understanding in terms of modernization. The activities of this group have not been favored by the government.[11]

The Islamic Movement of Uzbekistan, as its name indicates, is a movement originally formed by ethnic Uzbeks in the Ferghana Valley in 1991. Its objective has been the violent overthrow of the Karimov government and the establishment of sharia in Uzbekistan. It has metastasized into the larger Muslim world so that it carried out raids into the unstable country of Kyrgyzstan in 1999 and 2001. It also fought with the Taliban in Afghanistan.[12]. (Rather ironically, the Uzbeks in that country fought against the Taliban.)[13] Lately, it has joined the Taliban in Waziristan in a campaign to bring down the government of Pakistan. Initially, in the early and middle 1990s, under the name Adolat, it was tolerated and imposed sharia on much of the Uzbek section of the Ferghana Valley. But when it demanded that Karimov impose sharia on the whole country, Karimov cracked down.[14]

The Adolat movement supported the Islamic rebels in Tajikistan. Afterward, it transformed itself into the IMU and established links with Osama bin Laden and the Taliban. It was most active in 1999 and 2000, when, in addition to the forays into Kyrgyzstan, it conducted raids into Uzbekistan and Tajikistan. After 2001, the IMU was practically destroyed as a military force as the US supported government efforts (the US established military relations and aid with Uzbekistan, Tajikistan, and Kyrgyzstan after 9/11). As a result, since 2001 the IMU has been operationally inactive in Uzbekistan, but units continue to be active in both Afghanistan and Pakistan). It continues to be cited, however, for isolated terrorist incidents in Uzbekistan, Kyrgyzstan, and Tajikistan, and its main goal, even in a relatively dormant state, is to overthrow the current Uzbek government.[15]

Uzbekistan has had a tradition of Islamic reformism. In the early twentieth century, the country was a center of a movement called Jadidism. The Jadidists sought to reform Islam and Turkic culture through various means including aspects of modernity. The supporters were the upper middle classes and upper classes who had graduated from Russian and Turkish universities. Their emphasis was on secular education and other reforms meant to modernize the society. Although ultimately repressed, this movement still has supporters today. They also supported the Basmachi revolt of 1917–1920.[16]

The government has followed a two-pronged path in response to Islam. In 1998, it passed a law that prohibited people from worshipping in mosques not approved by and registered with the government. The official Council of Religious Affairs registers mosques and generally authorizes religious observances. Sermons are routinely monitored.

Religious leaders who do not preach officially approved versions of Islam are replaced. Occasionally, a suspect mosque is also closed. Religious literature is censored.[17.]

The approach to religious organizations that do not directly challenge the government can be quite benign. A prime example of this policy is the attitude to Sufis. As the Sufi have a tradition of tolerance and are not concerned with political aspects of Islam (as an internal devotional sect), they have earned government support. The most prominent recipient of government support is the Naqshabandi brotherhood, the largest Islamic *tarika*, or brotherhood, in the world.[18]

The central government has also countered the community roots of Islam through the mahalla community system, a Turkic tradition that dates back to the eleventh century. *Mahallas* are committees comprised of people living in the same area who share the same ethnicity. Usually presided over by elders, they conduct activities that combine local customs and Islamic traditions.[19]. The Karimov government has promoted this institution so heavily that currently there are over twelve thousand mahallas in the country.[20]

The Council of Religious Affairs approves and sometimes appoints the chairmen of the mahallas. Furthermore, in 1999, the Uzbek government created the new position of *posbon,* or neighborhood guardian, within the mahallas. These individuals are paid by the government and work with the police. They report back to the government on activities that take place in neighborhood mosques. Overall, they report back to the government on Islamic activities.[21]

The government can be considered an equal opportunity oppressor. It not only represses fundamentalist Islamic activities, it can also act against secular organizations. The main opposition party, the ERK or Freedom Party, is a political organization that supports nationalist expression. It has been persecuted and accused of terrorist activities. Its leaders have been subject to prosecution, and many have gone to the lengths of leaving the country.

Nonetheless, Uzbekistan has a rich cosmopolitan heritage. Even though the Ferghana Valley has a fundamentalist tinge, the country as a whole has a rich heritage of Muslim poets and philosophers. Its cities are living embodiments of past Islamic culture. The fabled khanates and modern cities of Tashkent, Bukhara, Samarkand, Khiva, and Kokand are living museums of past Muslim traditions. They are rich in architecture and mosques, traditional Islamic schools (makhtahs), Islamic seminaries (madrassas), ornate palaces from the past, and mausoleums of past Islamic rulers. Tashkent is noted for its mosques and madrassas, which date back centuries. Tamerlane made Samarkand his capital and the city also has ancient Muslim monuments. Bukhara's Muslim culture dates back for a millennium. Even today, it has over four hundred mosques and madrassas. It has been a center for Sufism. Khiva was a traditional center for the Great Silk Road, and Kokand is the religious center for the Ferghana Valley.[22] All of these cities, as well as several smaller urban centers, represent a vibrant Muslim past where learning, science, and the arts flourished. Even today, in spite of fundamentalism and the potential for violence, people continue to honor the past It is this tradition that continues to resonate today.

Kyrgyzstan: A Divided Mountain Nation

The Kyrgyz people are from a similar stock as the Kazakhs. The customs, traditions, and language are similar to the Kazakhs'. Before 1917 the Russians often called both groups Kyrgyz. Stalin distinguished between the peoples as the Kazakhs being people who occupied the steppes while the Kyrgyz lived in the mountains. Afterward, the two assumed their present separate identities.[1]

Kyrgyzstan is similar to most Central Asian countries in that the indigenous people have never been noted for religious zeal. Its geography and traditions have reinforced this distinction. Kyrgyzstan is extremely mountainous, and the majority of its people live in two areas: the Chu River Valley and its environs in the northern section, and the Ferghana Valley in the southeast, which it shares with Uzbekistan and Tajikistan. People in these areas make their living in different ways and adopted Islam at different times, with differing degrees of intensity, and maintain different ties with non-Kyrgyz people. In this last respect the Kyrgyz interact with the Tajiks and especially the Uzbeks in the Ferghana Valley, while the people of northern Kyrgyz interact with the southern sector of Kazakhstan.[2]

The land which became Kyrgyzstan has held its strategic position since Roman times when it was the northern sector of the Great Silk Root between China and Europe. The Kyrgyz arrived between the eleventh and thirteenth centuries. They originated near where the Kazakhs originated north of Mongolia and were and are Turkic speaking people who intermarried with Mongols. The southern Kyrgyz in the Ferghana Valley were gradually introduced to Islam between roughly 1200 and 1400. Islam spread more slowly into the northern region and really was not firmly established until the eighteenth century. During this period the Kyrgyz were dominated in the south by the Uzbek khanates such as Bukhara, Khiva, and Kokand, and they were somewhat oppressed. The northern part was often dominated by the Manchu (the governing group in China) until roughly the early1800s. As a result, the Russians were welcomed as liberators in the late eighteenth and early nineteenth century. After annexation to the czarist Russian empire, the country saw the arrival not only of Russians but of Ukrainians and eventually some Germans. These immigrants were awarded special privileges and brought a non-Islamic presence. Hence, it was not surprising that, like other Central Asian peoples, the native Kyrgyz joined the

Islamic-inspired Basmochi uprising, which was also caused by the intro-duction of conscription due to World War I between 1916 and 1920.[3]

The Soviets imposed atheism, but, as in other Central Asian coun-tries, there was subtle resistance. The Jadidist movement, which was described earlier, was prominent even before World War I, especially in neighboring Uzbekistan and elsewhere in Central Asia, including Kyrgyzstan. The movement promoted modernization and unity among Turkic-speaking peoples. Since independence there has been an upsurge of Islamic feeling.[4]

Along with the Kazakhs, many Kyrgyz maintain a nomadic lifestyle, even though many were forced into cities during the Soviet period. They combated the atheistic aspect of Soviet rule by the disguising of mosques and madrassas as opera houses, museums, and other tradi-tional cultural organizations. These changes were easy because Islam had long been intertwined with pre-Islamic customs. Even today, many people practice shamanism. They believe shamans link them with the spirit world as well as the hereafter. In rural areas people even believe that shamanism can predict the future and heal diseases brought in by evil forces. A large number of people also engage in animism as well as animal worship. Camels, owls, reptiles, and other creatures are often viewed as divine objects. In addition, a number of people worship the sun, moon, and other celestial objects as divine entities.[5]

Due to the post-independence departure of many Russians and other Europeans, the Kyrgyz are now a substantial majority in the country. Three quarters of them profess Islam today, so that the Islamic pres-ence is greater than ever. It continues to be a presence marked by large degree of interaction with traditional customs; even Islamic salvation has included the use of magic. , Two Muslim feast dates are associated with Turkic customs and continue to be practiced to this day: Kurban Ait, a day of remembrance on June 10, and Oroz Ait, celebrated at the end of Ramadan.[6]

At independence, the leaders who were former Communist func-tionaries were anxious to avoid overt acknowledgment of Islam. However, they were also anxious to reassure non-Kyrgyz who were still a significant part of the population and engaged in important techni-cal and industrial activities in a country that was still predominantly agricultural. Even today, a large number of those employed in technical occupations are non-Kyrgyz who do work that is crucial in a country still engaged in agriculture and where people still practice traditional customs and nomadic activities like stock-racing. As a result of these conflicting constituencies, a middle road has been adopted. The pre-amble to the constitution recognized the Muslim heritage which would be considered part of the national identity after independence, but the document went on to mandate a secular state by specifically prohibiting the intrusion of any ideology which would interfere with the business of state.[7]

Outside events have played a role in the country's relationship with Islam. The Iranian revolution and the Afghan struggle have affected the Kyrgyz. In fact, a substantial percentage of Kyrgyz live in what is today north Afghanistan, similar to both the Uzbek and Tajiks. The Kyrgyz also made similar defensive arrangements with the US after 9/11. Also, like the Uzbeks and especially the Tajiks, Kyrgyzstan has made defense arrangements with the Russians.[8]

Like Tajikistan, Kyrgyzstan has undergone tremendous economic privation. Inflation was so great (1200 percent in 1993 alone) that it has struggled. The country lost a market for its dairy products when the Soviet Union was dissolved. By 1999 the country had the highest public debt per population of any Central Asian state. Joblessness and poverty increased, as graduates of high school and colleges could not find work equal to their education. As mentioned earlier, a common challenge after Central Asia became almost completely literate during the Soviet period has been the development of an economy commensurate with K–12 and higher education.

The economic situation, combined with increasing political oppression in recent years, has led to a rise in militancy in a country that had been relatively tolerant and not overly zealous. The rise of extremism has accelerated in both the southern and northern parts of the country, with it being more apparent in the former and less in the latter. [9]

After independence the government attempted to show tolerance and acceptance to the Orthodox and other non-Muslim segments of the population, but as indicated before the government wanted to further its credentials as nationalistic through adherence to Islam, although hardly true believers in their private lives. In reality, there were special interests and financial aid from fellow Sunni Muslim states such as

Egypt, Turkey, and Saudi Arabia to encourage and support the government, which, despite the constitution's declaring the country secular, established a State Commission on Religious Affairs.[10]

In 1993 the government also established the Spiritual Administration for Muslims of Kyrgyzstan, or Samk.[11] Samk was meant to unite all Muslims in the country. It now embraces religious organizations, educational institutions, and mosques. Samk also initiated the publication of many religious brochures to familiarize readers with Islamic customs. It publicized religious scriptures and biographies of the prophet Mohammed. Today, Samk is comprised of several regional offices, an Islamic university, eight other institutions of higher learning ,and sixty-five madrassas and Koranic study classes. It trains clergy in the Qur'an and Haditha (the sayings of the prophet Mohammed), and also trains students in Islamic law and science. Samk maintains a liaison with various foreign religious societies and participates in international conferences and the construction of religious sites. Samk supervises most Islamic activity and coordinates all the activities of the mosques and madrassas in the country.[12]

The government has shown its support of Islamic activities by establishing religious newspapers in the capital city of Bishbek.[13] Other cities in the south, such as Osh and Jalal-Abad, also now have Islamic newspapers. As the south, especially the Ferghana Valley, is 95 percent Muslim, this is an important constituency.[14]

These activities have not prevented the country from becoming a target of Islamic extremist groups. The Islamic Movement of Uzbekistan, an Islamic radical association, made large-scale raids into both Tajikistan and Kyrgyzstan between 1999 and 2001. The country needed assistance from neighboring countries to ward off these attacks. These groups continue to be active, especially in the Ferghana Valley. The most prominent of these has been Hizb-ut-Tahir (HT), mentioned in previous chapters. Although it has denounced violence to achieve its aims, it is considered an incubator for more-violent groups. By 1999, it had organized in the Ferghana Valley so that it had three thousand members and overall had five thousand members in the country. It has now organized itself into ninety-three district and regional cells and has gained popularity through charitable contributions to poor families and its prison ministry.[15]

Earlier, Muslim countries had supported the building of mosques and madrassas. Support of Islamic associations also came from abroad. However, by 2001, the authorities had become alarmed.[16] Therefore, in 2003, the Turkistan Liberation Organization, a successor of the Islamic movement of Uzbekistan, as well as the East Turkistan Islamic party and the Islamic Party of Turkistan, were outlawed as sponsors of terrorism. Members of these organizations received short sentences under penal code Article 299 basically for insulting other religions' cultures through their activities, but after being released they have continued to operate in an underground manner. HT especially continues to recruit people in prison and to take advantage of the country's difficult economic situation. [17]

The activities of Saudi-supported Wahhabis were particularly incendiary, as they supported an intolerant, puritanical Islam. The previously tolerant and pluralistic Kyrgyz became alarmed again over the activities of these foreign-supported groups who were mostly in the Ferghana Valley, especially in the city of Osh, where they centered on mosques and madrassas. This city claims to be three thousand years old and has a place of pilgrimage called the mountain of Solomon, named after King Solomon.[18] Osh is home to an Islamic university, and most of its clergy are trained in Osh and the other major cities in the valley. The south, centered in the valley, is 95 percent Muslim, and its two largest groups, the Kyrgyz and Uzbeks, are Muslim. This area has a stricter adherence to Islam, and in Osh alone there are more than fifty mosques and nine madrassas [19] In the city of Jalah-Abad there are thirty-eight mosques.[20] People are often classified or classify themselves as true believers so as to differentiate themselves from the north. Especially in the economically depressed south, people tend to a more puritanical Islam, although there are more Uzbeks, who are stricter because they are nearly as numerous in the Ferghana Valley as the Kyrgyz. As a result, the treatment in some aspects is different in the north, particularly the role of women. Influenced by the zealous missionaries, especially from Saudi Arabia, southern women have taken to wearing the hijab and lead a more secluded life. There is opposition to abortion. Society in the valley, particularly among the Uzbeks, is more male-dominated than in the north.[21] The north is much more secular, tolerant, and pluralistic. In part, this reflects the past and presence of Russian and other European nationalities. There is a noticeable segment of Protestant as well as Buddhist missionaries. In the mountainous areas northeast of the capital and in the Chu Valley, pre-Islamic influences such as shamanism have continued to be strong. The presence of the officially secular government in Bishkek also puts a lid on extremism. Most industrial enterprises are now in the north, so it is not as economically depressed as the south, thereby removing another fertile ground for extremism.[22]

In general, despite the presence of Wahhabis and other extremist groups in the south, the fervor appears especially strong among Uzbeks and to some extent the Tajiks rather than the Kyrgyz. As yet, pan-Islamic feeling is not as strong as in some other countries. However, there is a strong pan-Turkic feeling among Kyrgyz. The government has sought to harmonize and cultivate the situation, but economic pressure and recent political upheaval in the country that has exacerbated tensions between Uzbeks and Kyrgyz in the Ferghana Valley have often served to aggravate religious feelings.[23]

As yet, however, the bulk of the people follow traditional aspects of Islam rather than the zealous puritanical version more prevalent in some parts of the south. This more traditional system is called often folk Islam and more or less involves a number of shamanistic activities that were practiced even before the arrival of Islam. Nevertheless, the difference of religious feeling among the ethnic groups, not just the Kyrgyz and Uzbeks but also the Tajiks and the Dungees, and other groups, has added an element of volatility into the mixture. Overall, though, the opposition to terrorism reinforced by the government does not make an extremist takeover imminent.[24]

A casual visitor to Kyrgyzstan, particularly the countryside, sees holy places called *mazars*. These mazars are an integral part of cultural religious purposes, as they include ancestor worship and visits to commemorate a shrine reminiscent of obedience to a departed saint, a custom of Sufism. In addition to traditional folklore, it includes visits to tombs and the worship of bushes, trees, rocks, and burial places linked to a historical or biblical personage. Of course, this custom reinforces the idea that God is everywhere, coupling animism with pantheism. Pilgrims often travel to hot springs to fulfill a vow or cure a sick relative, obtain a blessing, and even, for women, find a cure for infertility. Again, these practices are more common in the north than south.[25]

It should be emphasized that these folk customs now have not only a religious meaning, but they also have historical and aesthetic purposes in overall general cultural function. There is an overall indigenous quality about this which cannot be matched by outsiders, and this is also related to architecture constructed around mosques and madrassas and these sites. In general, these pilgrimage sites connect the country with the historical and cultural past, and often there are specific connections to nomadic and tribal customs. These traditions not only affect the Kyrgyz but also other Turkic peoples. For the Tajiks, this is often not because of ethnicity but also traditional religion among Iranian peoples.

Overall the custom of mazars has played multiple functions, and that explains its continued popularity and use among the people. It is a form of continuity with the past before Islam but also gained traction by identification with ancestors and the dead. The cult of the dead is part of the customs so prominent in the rural areas because there is a widespread belief that the dead pay visits, especially on Fridays. Women feel particularly welcome because as pilgrims they are treated equal to men, and in some parts of the country they are allowed in mosques in the same way so that when it comes to visiting shrines, they do not suffer discrimination. [26]

In general, when reviewing Islam and Kyrgyzstan, one draws several conclusions. First, religion remains popular as part of the folk tradition and culture. Second, religious fundamentalism has not penetrated the masses as yet because it is not connected with indigenous tradition. Finally, Islam is practiced in a way that emphasizes existing divisions in the country based on geographic, social, and economic aspects between north and south.

Concluding Comment

The states of Central Asia must deal with their past heritage. On the positive side, the Soviet era led to development and universal literacy. On the negative side, economic progress did not keep pace with these positive steps. The consequent disequilibrium has opened these newly minted states to forces which are potentially destabilizing.

Patterns of Islam in South Asia

Introduction

In South Asia, certain patterns of Islam are due to differences in topography. language, culture, and history. As has been noted elsewhere, these patterns created conditions that served to reflect syncretism stemming from group traditions and religions that pre-dated Islam. As in other parts of Asia outside of the Middle East, these patterns had additional influences from Sufism and religious orders. Furthermore, diverse ethno-linguistic groups added to Islamic patterns.

South Asia has additional ingredients which modify Islam. The countries under inspection are buffeted by regional and world forces that are often beyond their control.

Afghanistan has been the site of outside forces contending for influence. The Soviets tried to inculcate their values for over a decade. The Pakistanis encouraged the Taliban in an attempt to gain traction against its rival India in the subcontinent. The Taliban emerged from the South Asian (Pashtun) segments of the population and its opponents were backed by the Central Asian segments (Tajik, Uzbek, Kyrgyz, Turkmen). They were allies of the original al-Qaeda and its leader Osama bin Laden in the terrorism. NATO and the US intervened, so the war against Islamic terrorism is being carried out in Afghanistan.

This struggle has spread to Pakistan where the second largest group, the Pashtun, have shown sympathy with the Taliban as opposed to the largest group, the Punjabi, who are less fundamentalist. However, fundamentalist groups such as both the Wahhabis and Salafis have arrived in force within the world of Islam. They have also been active in other Islamic South Asian countries such as Azerbaijan and Bangladesh.

Moreover, tensions have increased between Sunni and Shia to the point of communal violence especially in Pakistan and Afghanistan. Sectarian violence among Muslims is aggravated by outside forces, with Saudi Arabia and, to some extent, Turkey supporting the Sunni while Iran supports the Shia. In Azerbaijan, these conflicts are even more complex, as Turkey not only supports the Sunni (along with the Saudis) but also follows a pan-Turkic agenda while Iran supports the pan-Islamic agenda. Only Bangladesh has escaped internecine warfare among Muslims, although it too has seen the arrival of fundamentalist groups. These countries all have or have had Islamic parties, but no Muslim party has ever exercised complete control.

One must also consider the ethnic diversity within most Muslim-dominated countries in South Asia. There is no majority group within either Afghanistan or Pakistan. Individuals within these countries have a tendency to identify with their ethnic group rather than with the designated nation. Thus, Pashtuns are self-identified and only secondarily may consider themselves Pakistanis or Afghans. In this way, Islam may be more of a binding force than citizenship in a created country. Conversely, large numbers of Azeris or Bengalis live outside their territorial borders. More Azeris live outside out Azerbaijan than within the designated boundaries of their country. Bengal has been split between a Hindu west and a Muslim east. This generated an irredentist element, the result of borders drawn by outsiders. Accordingly, Azeris would like to reunify with their brethren in Iran even though the Iranian Azeri have a stronger Shia element. Religion defined the creation of Bangladesh in spite of a traditional culture that united Hindu and Muslim. This section examines these above factors.

Afghanistan: Central Asia to South Asia

Afghanistan, or rather the territory on which it stands, has long been the gateway to the Indian subcontinent in South Asia. Historical routes such as the Khyber Pass and other mountain passes through the Hindu Kush Mountains have been routes of invasion and migration since the arrival in 1800–1500 BCE of the Aryans on their way to what became India and Iran, to Alexander the Great's invasion in the fourth century BCE, to Hunnic invasions in the fifth century CE, to the arrival of the Rajputs in the seventh century, to the Ghor and Ghazni invasions in the tenth and eleventh centuries, to the present.

The present entity of Afghanistan was founded in the eighteenth century and postdates the arrival of Islam in the seventh and eighth centuries. The country today is about 80 percent Sunni and the rest mostly Shia, similar to the configuration in most Muslim countries of Central and South Asia. In the northern portion of the country, about 40 percent of the population is in some ways a continuation of Central Asia, being composed of Tajiks (25 percent), Uzbeks (9 percent), Kyrgyz (5 percent), and Turkmen (1 percent). The southern and eastern sections are made up of Pashtun/Pathan speakers, who are also the second-largest group in Pakistan and make up the South Asian element in the population. They compose about 40 percent of the population and not only are the largest numerical group but also the most politically influential, furnishing the kings before the monarchy was overthrown in 1978, as well as most of the political leaders. The remainder of the population is mostly Shia, composed partly of the Hazara, a Mongol-descended group in central Afghanistan, and the population around Herat in the west of the country, both of which have been influenced by Iran. Much of Afghanistan is similar to Central Asia, with pre-Islamic customs, Sufism, and Sufi brotherhoods playing a large role in the popular exercise of religion. Islam in Afghanistan now contains both the *ulama*, or committee of religious scholars (whose position has declined in recent years), and the newly arrived extremists (over the past three decades), such as the Taliban and the Haqqani network.[1]

In village Afghanistan, *adat,* or custom, is quite common. More orthodox Islam, as represented by the sharia, is more prevalent in the urban areas (still a minority of the population). In tribal areas, the village religious person, or *mullah*, is not an official member of the clerical hierarchy, and he is appointed by the village, not the clergy. He usually concerns himself with rituals and can be paid by the village. His status varies with his education. He concerns himself with various religious rites such as baptism, marriage, burial, and the operation of the local Qur'anic school. He is considered a craftsman and, as such, can dispense both medicine and magical talismans to ward off evil. Quite often the tribal code prevalent in rural areas is at variance with strict Islamic law. Under tribal law, women are not allowed to inherit property, unlike under Islamic law; tribal law is more patrilineal. On the other hand, the repudiation of a wife is easier under sharia, whereas it would not happen in tribal society because it would be considered insulting to the woman's family. Vengeance can be pursued under tribal law, while the sharia limits this practice. Overall, the ulama is often considered a threat, as it represents an outside force.[2]

As in Central Asia and, in fact, much of Asia outside of the Middle East, Sufism plays an important role in Afghan Islam. It is so pervasive that many of the ulama are followers. Sufism is especially prominent among Muslims in the north and in and around the largest three cities of Kabul, Kandahar, and Herat, but is influential throughout the country. It appeals to many Afghans, as it stresses daily prayer by any individual as a form of mental discipline.[3]

Sufism is embodied by the three largest orders: the *naqshbandiyya*, the *quadiriyya*, and the *chishtiyya*. The first is the largest in the country and has several branches. The second is the only major Sufi order in the Middle East. The third is strong in the Indian subcontinent. The first is common in the north, while the other two are more common in the south. In South Asia, many members of Sufi orders follow a *pir*, or spiritual master. In Afghanistan, as elsewhere in South Asia, when a pir dies, a tomb is erected and becomes a shrine. Each of the three orders established its own madrassas. In the twentieth century, the government also established its own state-supported madrassas. This development, as well as the secularization of the legal system, led to the decrease of ulama influence in both education and law. Whereas the majority of Sunni ulama were educated in Pakistan, Shia ulama were educated at Qom in Iran and Najaf in Iraq. Extremism has crept in through the Deobandi school (see the later section in this chapter) and through Iran. However, as the only contingent area of Muslims lies around Herat, radical influence among Shia is limited to the 5 percent of the total population that live there.[4]

Fundamentalism takes the form of pushing the adoption of sharia law and the idea of a universal caliphate, or one Muslim state comprised of all members of the legal/political community, or umma. The idea of pan-Islamism has been espoused by the ulama and the Afghan government at different points in the twentieth century. The difference is that while fundamentalism means pushing basic concepts, Islamism put the emphasis on incorporating modern approaches to include technology which will enable a revived Islam to better confront foreign imperialism.[5]

The Deobandi movement, which dates from 1867, has been important, as most Afghans scholars have been educated at its seminary. The movement rejects innovation and supports Pan-Islam. It is fundamentalist but accepts Sufis (though not all of its practices, such as worship at shrines). Later movements that have entered Afghanistan, such as the Wahhabi and Islamist movements have followed this pattern. As it trained scholars from all ethnic groups, the Deobandi movement imparted a universality lacking in multiethnic Afghanistan. Ultimately, the Taliban received its training this movement there.[6]

Full-blown Islamism as a constant in Afghan Islam dates from late 1950s. Its main tenet was to establish a party of Allah which was to institute divine sovereignty through an Islamic government. In addition, besides the application of sharia law, the head of state should be chosen by Muslim precepts (as developed by the ulama). The emphasis is on the state itself, not the global caliphate. The stress was to be internal *jihad*—a constant struggle by the population against the falling back into ignorance. The application of *fiqh*, or the interpretation of sharia, followed the Hanafi school, which stated that the most the liberal of Muslim law codes were to be monitored, reinforced, and imposed on nonbelievers or traditionalists if necessary.[7]

The university intellectuals who started movements toward both fundamentalism and Islamism were reacting against what was termed excessive Western influence and the overly accommodationist Sufi and traditional elements of Islam. Ultimately, fundamentalism was absorbed by the more organized Islamism that originated in the more modern urban sectors of society between 1958 and 1965. Influenced by the Muslim Brotherhood of Egypt, this movement (Jamiat-e-Islam) was initially pan-Islamist. A more radical group founded by Gubuddin Hekmatyr (still active today and still virulently anti-Western) was Muslim Youth. It called for the overthrow of the total Afghan establishment.[8]

In general, Islamism in Afghanistan emerged from those aspects of Afghan society which felt most threatened by the outside world. Ironically, it was the most modern sector—the University of Kabul—which felt directly under attack from the West. Islamism never really became a mass movement in the countryside nor had general appeal until the reaction against foreign invaders—the Soviets from 1979 to 1989—and to some extent NATO since 2001. Overall, the strength of both Sufi tradition and traditional practices were a barrier. There was also no mass movement from the countryside to the city, which often is a fertile ground for Islamists because people feel adrift in a new, unfamiliar situation. External threats made people more receptive to Islamism as an adjunct of nationalism.[9]

It was the displacement, especially between 1979 and 1995—first resistance to the Soviets and then civil war between rival groups of muja-hedeen—which placed tribal elements, Sufis, and traditional believers in a refugee situation that led to radicalization. As Pashtun, Tajik, Uzbek, and Kyrgyz returned to their ethnic homelands, they became more sympathetic to radicals. The pluralistic Sufis, the scholarly ulama, and the syncretistic tribal believers were not as opposed as they had been to Islamist aims in terms of the sharia and advocacy against outside influence. The Pashtun, who spent the longest period as refugees, were especially propagandized.[10] Refugee camps were often run by Islamists and provided "free education" which served as recruiting tools. Pakistan, the host to about half of the refugees (fellow Pashtuns), was especially interested in gaining influence in Kabul as leverage against its rival, India. It was also undergoing a wave of Islamicization at this time under its leader, General Zia. The Pakistanis also were interested in pushing the Pashtuns, the second-largest group in Pakistan against ethnic rivals the Persian-speaking Tajiks, who might be more susceptible to Iranian influence. The struggle for power between various Islamic Mujahadeen, especially the Jamiat-e-Ulama and Muslim Youth, thus opened the way for the Taliban.[11]

Supported by the Pakistani National intelligence Service (the ISI), a group of young seminary graduates (predominantly Deobandi) (the Taliban) seized power in 1995–96.[12] In power, the Taliban sought to recreate a pure Islamic state. Men were ordered to keep their beards at a certain length and were punished for noncompliance. Minorities (non-Pashtuns) were often labeled non-Muslims and subject to attack. There were massacres of Shiites and persecution of Sufis. All modern conveniences were banned. Women especially were ill-treated. Unlike the Deobandi and other Islamist groups, which did not mandate restricted rights for women if they followed the sharia, the Taliban followed strict Wahhabi strictures, strict even by Wahhabi standards. All women were prohibited from leaving home without a male guardian. Women could not work outside the home (a major destabilizer in Afghanistan, where quite often women were the majority of professionals, particularly as physicians and teachers). In general, there were restrictions on women's access to health and education. The outcry was so great that the only Muslim countries to have any relations with the Taliban regime were Saudi Arabia, Pakistan, and the United Arab Emirates. When the Taliban was overthrown in November, 2001, there were few tears shed—at least in the non-Pashtun north.[13] If, as some forecast, the Taliban makes a comeback, it will be through force of arms, not the will of the people.

Nonetheless, the Islamic presence continues to permeate Afghan life, even if some the previous barriers to fundamentalism, such as Sufism and tribal beliefs, have suffered some attrition. Traditional political groups still survive, even if the dominant political forces revolve around pro- and anti-Karzai parties In the recent past, traditional groupings were divided into three categories—Islamists, traditionalists, and Shiites. There are three Sunni Islamist parties. The first is the successor group to the Muslim Youth group, the Hizb-i-Islami, still led by Hekmatyar. Its membership is comprised of graduates from government schools, as well as some ulama from the Kabul area. In spite of the latter, the members are mostly Pashtun. Its old rival, the Jamiyat-e-Islami, was until recently led by Burhanuddin Rabbani, the president of the country in the early 1990s, who was assassinated in 2011, allegedly by the Taliban. The Jamiyat-e-Islami is made up of graduates of government schools, the ulama from the north, and branches of the naqshbandiyya, also from the north. Today, its membership is mostly Tajik. It is a relative moderate party of Islamists. The final grouping, is a more moderate branch of the Hizb-i-Islami, called Khalis, and distinguished itself in the resistance to the Soviets. It is mostly Pashtun, but it has recruits from both the Kandahar and Kabul regions. As with the other two, it recruits from the government school.[14]

The second set of movements could also be termed traditional. The harakat-i-inquilab-i-islami is a moderate clerical party whose Pashtun ulama are educated at private madrassas. In contrast, the National Liberation Front is secular and gets its support from the old establishment, assorted tribes, and the Sufi order the naqshabandiyya. Finally, the Islamic Front supports the now defunct monarchy. Its membership is similar to the National Liberation Front, except it is more Pashtun and its Sufi sponsor is the Quadiriyya.[15]

The Shiite population, which constitutes 15–20 percent, also had three political groupings. The Hazara, a traditionally persecuted group, not too surprisingly supports the radical Islamist Shura-yi-ittifagh-i-islami. It is sponsored by Iran. Also radical Islamists supported by Iran are the Guardians of the Revolution. In contrast, the Harakat-i-islamia is a moderate Islamist movement and recruits from Shia that represent all ethnic groups.[16]

In spite of the swirling changes which have affected Afghanistan since 1978, folk or traditional Islam is still common in the countryside. It is still locally based although increasingly challenged by central authorities, whether muhajadeen or Taliban. The Sufi have also been rival loci of power in the three-handed area of Islamic authority. Generally, fundamentalism and especially Islamism has not made much headway in the countryside as opposed to the urban areas.

The continued strength of folk Islam, especially in rural areas, is its position as a guide to both social and moral behavior. Adherence to Islam conveys the idea of social and economic justice. Many people look on it as providing an ethical vision that protects them from the arrogance of power and general corruption. The Muslim hierarchy outside the urban areas which are more influenced by the state-controlled ulama is village-based. The village still remains the basic unit in Afghan society. As such, religious authority is based on the khan, alim, and mullah. The *khan* is the local landowner who has a large circle of dependents that can include the local religious authority. He can be the head of a clan or tribal sub-grouping, and he supports various communal activities, including religious celebrations. The *alim* is a local religious figure who has a higher educational degree beyond the madrassa, sometimes including a degree in Islamic law. He is often the highest religious authority in a given district (country or city). The state is gradually assuming control of the alim in the same way it assumed control of the ulama in the twentieth century (as part of a state hierarchy). The mullah's role in the village can sometimes overlap with both the alim and khan. The major point that must be emphasized is that Afghanistan continues to be a decentralized state and society, and therefore local authorities continue to exercise local authority, including religious authority, on a traditional basis.[17]

The continued violence in Afghanistan has weakened traditional sources of local authority. However, the central government has also been weakened. Nonetheless, the local hierarchy in religious affairs serves as a useful link between village link and capital, as do the Sufi, who, however weakened by fundamentalist and Islamist tendencies, still have some influence due to their emphasis on individual meditation over worldly power.[18]

Currently, the Afghan government supports the separation of church and state on a constitutional basis but seeks to emulate Turkey, where Islam plays a key role. Islamism has not enjoyed a wide appeal beyond certain urban areas and the middle class because it has sociopolitical aims—a state run by sharia and, in the fundamentalist version, a return to the Islam of the seventh century, with only the necessary accommodation to modernity to function. The other aspects include the primary role of the Qur'an and Haditha, and a pan-Islamic universal state comprised of members of the umma.[19] Most Afghans continue to be good Muslims, but their emphasis is on personal ethics and morality rather than worldly power, which many equate with oppression and corruption.[20]

As Afghanistan modernizes and becomes more attuned to the outside world, change will be inevitable. Certainly ethnic and folk traditions in polyglot Afghanistan will continue to be strong as the concept of "Afghanistan" continues to be weak. Inevitably, village traditions will be weakened as technology penetrates formerly isolated villages and regions. The new interaction will alter the pattern of Islamic observance. The basic goal for the state is to integrate private practices of Islam with the requirements of a modern state. The ideal polity should include practicing Muslims enclosed in a state that looks to the future while it honors the past.

Azerbaijan: Between Asia and Europe

Azerbaijan is in the southern part of the Caucasus right across from its Turkic kinsmen on the eastern side of the Caspian Sea, which borders Azerbaijan. Technically, it straddles the border between Asia and Europe. The policy of the government has been to identify with Europe by seeking admission to the European Union and strengthening its contacts with the West.[1]

At the same time, Azerbaijan is located between the Caspian and Black Seas, historically a sort of turnstile for maritime traffic, with connections to the Great Silk Road. More significantly, it has been the land bridge for both north-south and south-north migrations and invasions. After 2000 BCE, people from Central Asia and the steppes north of the Caucasus Mountains invaded the ancient Near East and established the Hittite and the Assyrian empires in central Anatolia and northern Mesopotamia, respectively. After 800 CE, Turkic speakers, mostly the Oghuz confederation, used the area as an invasion route into the Middle East. Invasion also came from the opposite direction. Persian speakers invaded the area several times between 600 BCE and 600 CE. Islam was also brought from the South by Arabs in the late seventh century. Both Alexander the Great and the Roman Empires included the area in their empires.

In the process, Azerbaijan has undergone several identity changes which underline its border status. Its Christianity dates from 100 CE while its nominal overlord, the Roman Empire, was still pagan. The Persian interlude introduced Zoroastrianism into the country, and remnants of both still exist. Islam dates from 650, and the country has been preeminently Shiite since 1500. The ancient inhabitants were called Albanians, whose ethnicity has not been established. The ethnic identity changed after the Turkic invasion in the ninth and tenth centuries. Today, a Turkic dialect most closely identified with Turkmenistan and Turkey is spoken.[2]

Most modern Azeris consider themselves as part of the Turkic family. Others maintain that they are related to Persian speakers who have been Turkified.[3] A similar process occurred in Bulgaria where the Bulgars, who were originally a Turkic group, became Slavicized through language and religion.

Azerbaijan is being pulled in several directions. It is geographically between Europe and Asia. Its neighbors to the west, Georgia and Armenia, are Orthodox Christian (although Azerbaijan has had a century-old dispute with the latter, most recently over the border area of Nagorno-Karabakh), but Iran and Turkey, to the southeast and southwest, are Muslim. Also, the country has been divided since 1828, with present-day Azerbaijan having a population of 8 million, while 18 million to the south are now part of Iran, where they constitute nearly one quarter of the population, second only to Farsi-speaking Persians.[4]

Typical of a border state, Islam has not been a predominant factor for the non-Iranian portion of the Azeri figure, unlike their Iranian kinsmen. Rather, their identity has been more with traditional Turkic culture than with Islam. Islam is considered part of the national identity but does not define it. In addition, the multi-confessional heritage of the country plus decades of atheistic Soviet rule that furthered dampened religious zeal has tended not to support widespread fundamentalist feeling (although since the breakup of the Soviet Union, there has been a fundamentalist party, the Islamist Party of Azerbaijan).[5]

Azerbaijan intermingles religion with custom. Despite a population that is 93 percent Muslim, the Azeri constitution permits every faith to practice its religion. These include Russian and Armenian Orthodox Christians, as well as pockets of Judaism and Zoroastrianism.[6]The Muslim population is divided into about 75 percent Shia and the remaining Sunni. The Sunni appear to be increasing in population. Currently, the Shia predominate in the south, and the Sunni are predominant in the north. The south is influenced by Iran across the border, while the north is influenced by Sunni Turkey. Cognizant of this division, the administrative Muslim Spiritual Board of the Transcaucasus headquartered in Baku divides its leadership. Its chairman is Shia, while the deputy is Sunni. [7]

In general, fervor is relatively low. Less than one tenth of Azeri consider themselves to be devoted Muslims. In part, this is a heritage from Soviet times. Unlike their coreligionists, the Azeri did not find ways to practice their religion clandestinely. As an example of this, Azeri Shia celebrate Ashura, the most holy day of the Shia calendar which centers the martyrdom of Hussein in 680. Devout Muslims stress the religious connotations, while others, including most Shia, see Islam as part of folklore and Ashura as a symbol for survival against overwhelming odds—a thinly veiled analogy to Soviet times when religion was repressed.[8]

Islam staged a combat the end of the 1980s, when there were fewer than seventy mullahs. There were so few clerics that a mullah would often perform both Sunni and Shia ceremonies. Since independence in 1991, both Iran and Turkey have sent missionaries, which aided in a revival of Islam.[9] Soon, however, the missionaries overplayed their hand. The Islamic Party of Azerbaijan openly followed the lead of its benefactor, Iran, and advocated the establishment of an Islamic republic. The Azeri authorities soon became suspicious that the party was spying for Iran and outlawed it. Since then, all missionaries must register with the Spiritual Board in order to visit local communities. In addition, the number of missionaries and the length of their stay are now limited.[10]

Fundamentalism has not been very successful in Azerbaijan due to the tradition of relative tolerance based on pluralism. For two thousand years, it had a thriving Jewish community in its midst, and until recently. There were good relations with Orthodox Christians. In this respect, the fight over Nagorno-Karabakh (an Armenian enclave within Azerbaijan), which has been invaded and occupied by the Armenians, did cause outbreaks in Baku, the capital of Azerbaijan. These attacks were directed against Armenians as a group rather their religion.[11]

Pan-Islamism has had to contend with pan-Turkism. The latter seeks to unite Turkic or Turkic-speaking peoples from Central Asia, Turkey, and Azerbaijan. Pan-Islamism was represented early in the twentieth century by the Musavat Party, which advocated Muslim unity and independence. The Bolshevik Revolution led to much bloodshed and ultimately its suppression in 1920, after brief independence between 1918 and 1920. The Soviets sought to eradicate all sources of nationalism and replaced the Arabic alphabet first with the Latin alphabet (1924) and then with the Cyrillic alphabet (1940). After independence, the Latin alphabet was reintroduced.[12]

Azeri sentiments are similar to Central Asia in the tying of religion to culture, or in some cases to pre-Islamic customs. As an example, one can point to the favorite Azeri holiday of Novruz, which has been celebrated for nearly three thousand years in connection with vernal equinox on March 21. It is rooted in the Zoroastrian religion and is a remnant of Persian culture, when their relatives the Medes started to filter into the area in the first millennium BCE. Although Ramadan is observed, Novruz, or "new birth" is far more popular.[13]

Today, Islam rather than Islamic fundamentalism is more prevalent. Even though Azerbaijan borders Iran, which has two thirds of the ethnic Azeri population and is the epitome of Shiite fundamentalism and has engaged with Christian Armenia in a long-running dispute, Azerbaijan has steered a middle course. This is particularly impressive as it borders the Caucasus Mountains on the south. This volatile region has seen Muslim-inspired uprisings against and Christian /Muslim communal strife in Dagestan, Chechnya, and Ingushetia. Neighboring Orthodox Christians have seen Muslim revolts in the provinces of Abkhazia and South Ossetia.[14]

Given these factors, there has been very little violence arising from religion in the country. Outwardly, Islam has blossomed in the republic after independence as new mosques and madrassas were built. Young Azeri travelled overseas to Islamic institutions of higher learning in Iran, Turkey, Saudi Arabia, Egypt, and Pakistan. Azeri leaders have routinely gone on religious pilgrimages. Yet in spite of these manifestations of religious feelings, in a recent survey, only 17.7 percent of respondents indicated that they observed the Muslim injunction of daily prayer.[15]

The relationship between government and Islam has undergone different phases in the post-independence period. In the initial phase, secular nationalists and observant Muslims cooperated in the struggle for independence. At this stage, political parties contented themselves with the maintenance of Islam as a strictly ethical and religious element in social life, not political life. During this period, the Law of Freedom of Religion was adopted. All religious property that had been taken during the Soviet era was restored. The Spiritual Department was separated from the state, and all state assistance to the department was ended. All clergy were henceforth to be paid by public donations. Freedom of worship was inaugurated.[16]

The second phase came with the present regime. Anxious to gain legitimacy, the regime's new president, Heydar Aliyev, swore fidelity to both the constitution and the Qur'an. In return, the supposedly independent Spiritual Department now began to give all government actions its stamp of approval and devoted itself to propaganda on behalf of the government. Aliyev's son and successor, who took over after his death in October, 2003, has continued his father's policies.[17]

The attitude toward other forms of religious expression has been quite different. The radicalism of the Islamic Party of Azerbaijan, as well as the radicalism of certain missionaries, led, as we have seen, to the outlawing of the first and the limiting of the other. However, alternates to "official Islam" continue to be active. Wahhabi/Salafi missionary activity has continued. The Salafis in particular have been active, and by 2003 had sixty-five mosques in the country [18] By 2006, membership in Wahhabi/Salafi organizations was over twenty-five thousand. Overall, through the efforts of these groups and government support, the number of mosques increased in two decades from fewer than seventy to fourteen hundred.[19] Nevertheless, although the Wahhabi/Salafi groups have not been proscribed, they are subject to arrest. Other radical fundamentalist organizations such as Hezbollah are closely monitored. Unlike official Islam, these organizations are anti-Turkic, anti-Semitic, and anti-American. They look on nationalistic religion as *shirk*, or anti-Islamic, and a violation of monotheism.[20]

In spite of the above and the continued activity of radical missionaries, especially from Saudi Arabia and Iran, Islam remains rather shallow, as public knowledge about basic rituals continues to be rather limited. Syncretism with Turkic customs and pre-Islamic religions continues unabated. Fortunetellers use the Qur'an, for instance, to foretell the future. Many Shia believe the tenth day of Muharram (a holiday which involves whipping and self-flagellation) is the most important ceremony in Islam (ignoring Eid and Ashura), since they do not pray or follow basic precepts of Islam. Often lines for basic rituals (funerals and marriages) are not recited, as some mullahs still do not know them.[21]

Most Azeri continue to view Islam as part of their national identity. They also continue to reject the mixture of religion and politics propagated by religious radicals. Islam is a national characteristic just as the Turkic language and culture are. Accordingly, no single group can claim a special status.[22.]

So indifferent are Azeri to the performance of Islamic duties that Azerbaijan, alone among Islamic countries, does not fill the quota allotted to countries to make the pilgrimage to Mecca. Instead, vacant places are sold to pilgrims from Chechnya and Dagestan. Many Azeri also reject the wearing of garments that signify religion.[23]

Azerbaijan is a moderate secular country. Nevertheless, sectarian differences can lead to tension. The Iranian influence on Shiites in the south is counterbalanced by Salafist (most from Egypt) in the north among Sunni. Although the country as whole is not zealous when it comes to religion, fundamentalist groups such as the Salafists can be appealing as they preach a universal message that transcends sects. They also benefit from discontent with the government whose leadership is considered both autocratic and corrupt by many Azeri. In this respect, not much of the country's wealth in oil and gas has filtered down to the masses.[24]

External events have increased dissatisfaction with the government. The presence of coreligionists such as Chechens has increased ill feeling. Furthermore, the Armenian conquest of Nagorno-Karabakh (a mostly Armenian enclave which had been placed under Azeri administration during the Soviet period) led to the arrival of several hundred thousand refugees in Azerbaijan. This event was attributed to governmental incompetence. The feeling that official Islam is an arm of government has further embittered the population. [25]

Overall, there is a feeling that there has been a general decline in morality and ethics. Newly arrived Islamists and fundamentalists therefore find a ready audience. In addition, young Azeri educated abroad have been exposed to radical ideas, both fundamentalist and Islamist. They bring these ideas with them when they return to Azerbaijan. If these trends continue, the general secular orientation of Azerbaijan may change.

Pakistan: Concept or Country?

Pakistan holds a unique distinction in the Muslim world. It is the only country in today's world created solely to accommodate the Islamic religion. It means "land of the pure" in Urdu, the official language of the country. It can also function as an amalgam of the country's largest ethnic groups. It is the major bonding element for the Punjabis, Sindhis, Pashtun, Baluchi, and Kashmiris.[1] Islam came to the Indian subcontinent, including today's Pakistan, through trade with the coastal province of Sind in the early eighth century. Later invasions from Central Asia in the tenth and eleventh centuries brought Islam to Kashmir and the Pashtun (today the Northwest Territories in Pakistan, plus adjoining areas in Afghanistan) territories.[ ] They were the springboard to Muslim rule in northern India (the Delhi Sultanate as well regional states), which culminated with the Mogul Empire (1526–1707) which ruled over much of India and culminated in the conversion of many Indians, especially in the Punjab and the Indian part of Baluchistan to Islam. During its heyday, it was considered of the great gunpowder Islamic powers along with the Ottoman Empire (Turkey) and the Safavid Empire (Persia). It lasted technically until 1858, when the British formally took over and assumed the authority they had privately exercised for a century.[2]

The creation of modern Pakistan was presaged by the formation of the Muslim League in 1909 to protect Islamic interests in the subcontinent. By 1930, Mohammed Al-Jinnah and Allama Muhammad Iqbal were promoting the idea of a Muslim state formed out of India. In 1940, the Muslim League in the Lahore Resolution officially called for a separate state. Communal violence increased as the 1940s wore on, and the British came to support the idea of partition upon independence, which took place in August, 1947. Each province was to choose accession to either India or Pakistan. However, in two cases, the ruler ignored the wishes of his subjects. In Kashmir, it was a Hindu ruler who ignored the wishes of the Muslim majority and acceded to India. As a result, fighting occurred between August, 1947, and December, 1948. A ceasefire gave about one third of Kashmir to Pakistan, but it has since been a source of contention, including at times military conflict.[3] The precise role of Islam has been a matter of debate since the founding of the state. There were advocates for a liberal secular state, but the constitution that was eventually adopted in 1956 declared Pakistan an Islamic republic, although it allowed freedom of worship. The 1971 separation of East Pakistan (now Bangladesh), due to the intervention of India, led to increased unrest in West Pakistan (now Pakistan). Military rule has alternated with civilian rule in Pakistan's history, and the seizure of power by Muhammad Zia ul-Haq (1977–88) led to increased power for Islam in the country. Under his rule, the national assembly abolished many laws that did not confirm to sharia. Islamic criminal laws were adapted. Zia set up the Islamic Council, which was established to review all extant laws for conformity to Islam.[4] Zia also enacted further measures to increase Muslim principles, such as interest-free banking and the revision of school textbooks to include more Islamic content. Government officials were encouraged to persuade people to pray five times a day.[5]

Today, 97 percent of people in Pakistan are Muslims, with 77 percent Sunni and 20 percent Shia. Pakistan has two small sects, the Ismaili sect and the Ahmadiya sect (which is considered an offshoot of Islam, but not by many other Muslims among its nearly 200 million). As in other parts of Central and South Asia, Sufism is popular among both Sunni and Shia. Sufis believe that one can come close to G-d through dance, poetry, music, and meditation. Some people belong to religious orders or fraternities, but most observe Sufi rites individually. As in other parts of Asia outside of the Middle East, holy men, or *pirs,* are quite common. After death, tombs of these pirs become shrines visited by many who were devoted to the pir in life. These visitors pray, leave offerings, and celebrate festivals at the site.[6]

Muslims do exercise influence in electoral and judicial spheres in Pakistan. In the General Assembly, 207 of 217 elected seats are reserved for Muslims. Although there is a secular Supreme Court, all matters related to Islam are referred to a religious court called the Federal Shariat (sharia) Court. Three of the four major political parties are avowedly religious. They include the venerable Muslim League, the Islamic Democratic Alliance, and the Islamic Assembly. The federal capital built in 1961 to be the seat of government is called Islamabad, literally "city of Islam."[7]

As in other Muslim countries, traditions and customs permeate Islam in Pakistan. Overall, though, most Muslims believe that it is their duty to teach children the rituals and basic beliefs of Islam. Therefore, madrassas dominate the secondary school horizon, and government schools emphasize Islam in their curriculum. Many women, especially in the countryside, still practice *purdah*, or seclusion, or only appear in public with their faces covered.[8]

Currently, the fundamentalist and Islamist element is represented by the Pakistan branch of the Taliban ;(which was at least partially created by the Pakistani Intelligence Service). After 9/11, Pakistan became ground zero in the war against Islamic terrorism. Both the Afghan and Pakistan Taliban are centered in the Pashtun/Pathan (the Northwest Provinces of North and South Waziristan and Chitor), areas which are the ethnic homelands of the Taliban. They are autonomous, and the leading party in this area, the fundamentalist party Jamiat-e-Ulema-Islam (JUI) was founded here. The JUI derives from the Deobandi movement, which also trained most Taliban students. This movement, although much smaller in numbers than its rival, the more moderate, Punjab-based Barelvi, has had an outsized influence on Pakistan, Afghanistan, and Central Asia, as it controls the great majority of seminaries in Pakistan. It has worked in tandem with Saudi Arabia, which supports it financially because it resembles the Wahhabi in its major tenets. The JUI puts loyalty to religion above loyalty to any country and says that the basic right of any Muslim is to fight any non-Muslim or apostate in another country. It criticizes Sufis and Shia as being non-Muslim. It is against any prominent role for women and Western influence. Many of its positions were adopted by the Taliban, who, during their rule in Afghanistan, were especially outspoken against women outside the home and against Shia. The JUI has somewhat modified its anti-Sufi rhetoric as it realizes the influence that Sufism plays in Pakistan. It does, however, continue to emphasize the primacy of the Qur'an and the Haditha (sayings of the Prophet). Along with other Central and South Asian Muslims, the Deobandi support the Hanafi law code. Their messianic message has also been disseminated by ulama scholars, many of whom trained at its seminaries.[9]

Today, Pakistan is considered a center of fundamentalist terrorist activity. Osama bin Laden was sheltered there, and it is reportedly the hiding place of his successor, Anwar Zawahiri, as well as the deposed head of the Afghan Taliban, Mullah Omar. The attacks of American drones against Al-Qaeda and Taliban sanctuaries, however effective militarily, have increased anti-American feeling. This is unfortunate, as the majority of Pakistanis are non-fundamentalist and many are secular. There is a sliding scale of religious extremism, with the Pashtun/Pathan being the highest and the Punjabi—the most numerous group, with close to 50 percent of the population and close to 60 percent including offshoots—being the least fundamentalist. The other groups, Baluchis, Sindhi, and Muhajirs (Indian Muslim emigrants) fall in between. The conflict against Islamic extremists via drone attacks and other military operations has produced a degree of sympathy for these groups they would otherwise not enjoy. In some ways, the rationale for Pakistan among Muslims has come full circle. In the 1940s, the Muslim League presented a picture of the "land of the pure which would transcend sectarian, regional, and linguistic differences." [10] The campaign against Muslim extremists may now produce the opposite effect by uniting the country against external interference.

A source of tension in the region is the continued suspicion on the part of the Afghan, Central Asian, and Indian governments that the Deobandi movement, the JUI party, and the Pakistan Intelligence Service may be continuing to support radical fundamentalist movements such as Islamic Movement of Uzbekistan, the Haqqani movement, and the Taliban. The Pakistani government has promised to curb links between Pakistan parties and militants, and also to forbid militants from attending madrassas, including those run by the Deobandi. But countries such as India and the United State are still skeptical, as they believe the promises have not been kept. Terrorism continues against Indian Kashmir, and the recent Mumbai attack was organized from Pakistan. The United States still harbors suspicion that the sheltering of Bin Laden could not have occurred without the complicity or knowledge of Pakistani officials.[11]

This suspicion of a country which receives approximately two billion dollars in aid annually from the United States and has a tradition of some secularism and some degree of moderation may appear surprising. But for many years, except for a period of time (the rapprochement began later in the decade and took off after 2001) when the United States cut off aid after Pakistan exploded a nuclear device in 1990, there was a confluence of interests. Pakistan and the United States allied to confront Communist influence in the region and supported efforts by the Afghan fighters to combat the Communist or pro-Communist regime(s) in Kabul in 1979–1989. There was also activity against the Soviets in Central Asia. Pakistan wanted assistance against its regional (and stronger) rival, India. The United States went along because for many years (until the 1980s), India was seen as pro-Soviet. The last three decades have seen a change as India has boomed through procapitalist activity. Rivalry with China has drawn the United States and India closer, and they collaborate in both the security and economic realms. Ironically, and perhaps inevitably, Pakistan has drawn closer to China. Moreover, domestic politics dictate a certain degree of forbearance toward pro-fundamentalist segments of the population, as no political party wishes to alienate them totally.[12]

Today, Islam is the official religion of the "Islamic Republic of Pakistan." Originally, though, the precise role of Islam in the newly created state was debated. The first leader and founder, Mohammed Al Jinnah, spoke of a place where Hindu and Muslim would find their identity as common citizens of one state so that Islamic laws would not be applied (a direct nod to secularism). A common civil code was enacted based on the English model. The first constitution indicated that "the state would submit to the sovereignty of God." The ulama wanted the law to strictly follow the dictates of sharia. This was rejected. [13]

Over the years, political changes did strengthen the role of Islam. As discussed earlier, President Zia increased the standing of Islam. Just before he was overthrown, his predecessor, Ali Bhutto, had outlawed the use of alcohol and drugs. Zia attempted to make sharia the law of the land. The independent judiciary blocked this, and the compromise ruled that laws which affected every individual in society were not within the venue of sharia unless the law was proved to be "un-Islamic." A welfare taxation system based on the Qur'anic injunction of *zakat* began. A new system of banking was initiated based on the prohibition against usury or charging of unjust interest. Nevertheless, the constitution in force in Pakistan today states that only a Muslim can hold office as president or prime minister. As explained earlier, no law considered inimical to Islam can be made or ratified, and all existing laws must be compatible with Islam.[14]

In spite of these provisions, no party based solely on Islam has ever captured a majority of seats in the parliament (national assembly and senate), although Muslim parties have held power with external support. Pakistan is a very large country, with a population approaching 200 million (the sixth in the world). As a result, one cannot make generalizations about the country, volatile though it is. Outwardly, Pakistan appears uniform with an estimated 95–97 percent of the population identified as Muslim. However, there are almost 40 million Shia in that 165 to 170 Muslim population. Although communal violence has grown in recent years (in part inspired by Deobandi ideas), Shia have played an important role in the nation's history. The nation's founder, Mohammed Al-Jinna, and his chief aide, Khaunja Nazimiddun, were Shia. The Bhuttos, Asif Ali Zamdari, Yahya Khan, and Iskander Mirza, as well as other prominent political and military leaders, were Shia.[15] Pakistan is really the only Sunni-majority country where Shia have been elected to high office and played an important role in nation-building. Although there have been clashes increasing in intensity the past few years, most inspired by fundamentalists (there are also periodic clashes among the rival Muslim movements of the Sufi-friendly Barelvi and the anti-Sufi Deobandi), the Shia still have a great deal of clout. Their numbers alone make them a political force in elections. When General Zia tried to introduce zakat, the Shia protested and were exempted. They have succeeded in introducing a separate curriculum for Shia students in public school. The Shia have developed their own organizations, such as USO, to defend their own interests, and they now have their own militant groups to oppose Sunni radical groups. [16]

In a country as culturally diverse as Pakistan, there are a variety of religions. There are millions of Christians, Hindus, Zoroastrians, and Baha'i. There are also offshoots of both Shia and Sunni. The most famous Shia offshoot is the Ismaili sect, identified with the Aga Khan. The most prominent Sunni offshoot is the Ahl-Haditha, related to the Salafi movement. The Ahmadiya (which, as mentioned above, also exists in Southeast Asia) has often been considered non-Muslim by orthodox Muslims, although it considers itself Islamic. The Ahmadiya believe that Mohammed is the last and best of the prophets but not the final word.[17] Its relationship with Islam is perhaps analogous to the relationship of the Church of Jesus Christ of Latter Day Saints with mainline Christianity.

Even though the Deobandi and other fundamentalist such as the JUI organizations receive an inordinate amount of attention, they are still a minority among Muslims. Both Shia and Sunni have more grounds of agreement than differences. They both belong to Sufi organization and the related brotherhoods.[18]

There are other organizations and forces that emphasize moderation. Most Deobandi (like other Sunni Muslims) belong to the Hanafi school of jurisprudence, a relatively inclusive school. Even some members of the Deobandi belong to Sufi organizations, as the idea of personal communion with Allah and meditation has crossover appeal. In the rural areas, many Muslims commingle Islamic observance with pre-Islamic and non-Islamic customs.[19]

The greatest impediment to fundamentalism is the pro-Sufi Barelvi movement, which represents 50 percent of Sunni or close to 80 million people. Starting with opposition to the Wahhabis, the Barelvi has taken a stand against hard-line ideology and defended Sufi and even traditional religious folk customs. Overseas, it has even defended visits to shrines, including the tomb of the wife and daughter of the Prophet. In this case, it has gone against the wishes of the host government, Saudi Arabia, which has taken the Wahhabi view that visits to the tomb are idolatrous.[20]

The Barelvi group was active against Afghan and Pakistani Taliban because of their use of violence and broad use of the jihad. The Barelvi movement is also the main force in the Sunni United Council, an amalgam of eight movements from South Asia organized to combat extremism. These movements have also formed the Save Pakistan Movement as a force against Talibanism (and indirectly, the Deobandi).[21]

The role of Islamic (Sufi) brotherhoods is also important. They tend to be constructive, opposed to political activism, and active in social welfare activities. They support traditional practices such as organized visits to shrines of deceased Sufi pirs and other holy figures. The membership in these orders is in the millions, including both Sunni and Shia and thus serving an ecumenical purpose. The most active brotherhoods are the Naqshbandiyya, Quadiriyya, Chishtiyya, and Suhrawdiyya, As discussed earlier, the first two are global organizations present throughout Asia.[22]

There is also increasing secularism in this populous nation which is rapidly modernizing and urbanizing, two forces that resist fundamentalism. In spite of laws on the books prohibiting alcohol and drugs, these laws are often ignored among the young, especially in the city. The social taboos against the intermingling of the sexes are also largely ignored by the urban young. Pakistan is now 50 percent urbanized, and some of the social structures are not so easily enforced in large heterogeneous populations.[23]

In spite of modernization, the forces of orthodox Islam have enlisted education to reinforce Islam. The study of Islam is now compulsory through the tenth grade in government schools. Madrassas have proliferated and are now available to impoverished youth who cannot afford the fees related to government schools. Opportunities to go on pilgrimages—often subsidized—to Mecca and Medina have encouraged the development of pan-Islamic feeling. The use of Islamic media for the reading of the Qur'an and other sacred scriptures have tended to crowd out traditional folk beliefs and practices in mass communications.[24]

If present demographic projections hold, Pakistan is on the way to becoming the largest Muslim country in the world. Should it continue on the traditional path wherein Sufi, Hanafi, and Barelvi organizations promote a less dogmatic model? Alternately, will it go the way of fundamentalism due to a variety of factors such as popular resentment of drone attacks and increased aggressiveness of the Deobandi as well as the Wahhabi and Salafi movements, encouraged by occasional acts of the government? Only the future can tell! Although the traditional belief systems associated with folk Islam may be under attack by fundamentalist purists, the power of popular belief is still evident whenever a pir passes on and masses of believers turn out.

A Culture and a Nation: Bangladesh

Bangladesh is a country whose reason for existence has been determined by religion. As a result of the Partition of India in 1947, the Muslim eastern section of historic Bengal voted to join the newly created Pakistan. It became known as East Pakistan. In 1971, feeling exploited by the western section (now known as Pakistan), it broke away with Indian assistance to form the present nation of Bangladesh. It has been Islamized since the period of 1200–1500. During this time, the inhabitants of eastern Bengal—mostly composed of non-Aryans, low-caste Hindus, and aboriginal tribal people—gradually converted to Islam.[1] Today, the country is nearly 85 percent Muslim, with the remainder being mostly Hindu. With over 150 million people crowded into 55,000 square miles, it is the most densely populated country in the world. It is also the third-largest Muslim country in the world in terms of population.[2]

Sufism, as in other parts of the Asian Muslim world, is quite popular in Bangladesh, partly due to Hindu and Buddhist influence in traditional Bengali culture, and the Sufi concept of pursuing the truth with a spiritual guide or teacher called a *pir* or *fakir*. The fakir is considered an itinerant holy man, while a pir is considered to be at a higher spiritual level.

In Bangladesh, Sufism is so ingrained that there is a hierarchy attached to members. There are disciples but also associates. The disciples are associates who live in a secular environment. The associates can include devotees to shrines and people who practice pious exercise in order to receive mystical enlightenment. The Sufi orders are also prominent. They include the Naqshbandiyya, Quadiriyya, and Chishtiyya. The first two are worldwide.[3]

As elsewhere, there is a community of religious scholars who administer and interpret religious laws. They are divided into *maulvis*, *imams*, and *mullahs*. The first two terms are often used interchangeably. They both conduct services in the mosques and madrassas. The maulvi, though, is an imam who has had further studies at a school of religious education.[4] Mullahs are often local clerics whose duties involve both orthodox religious ceremonies, such as marriages and funerals, and other duties that reflect folk customs rather than Islamic rituals. They give special amulets and tokens for a variety of maladies ranging from snakebite to impotence. All of these objects are meant to provide good luck and protection against evil spirits.[5]

The practice of pir worshipping is quite common in the Indian subcontinent among Muslims. The additional factor here is the strong admixture of Hindu elements, which forms part of local syncretism. The Hindu elements are common in ceremonies such as Shab-e-barat, or the Festival of Lights. This is derived from the Hindu festival of lights. Moreover, people in Bangladesh have borrowed the custom of jinns (magical spirits) to exorcise demons and other evil spirits. So complete is the Muslim-Hindu synthesis, particularly in rural areas, that Muslims do not distinguish between Hindu and Muslim temples when they engage in religious observance. Synthesis is also apparent in attendance at shrines typical of both religions. Muslims have a supernatural deity for the treatment of cholera derived from a Hindu concept.[6]

Since the 1970s, government involvement in religious affairs has increased. After independence, the constitution of Bangladesh established Islam as a state religion. It also guaranteed freedom of religion. In 1988, the government encouraged the parliament to pass a constitutional amendment which made Islam the state religion.[7] After independence, the government established the Ministry of Religious Affairs, which provided financial support for aspects of observance such as community prayer grounds and mosques. It also took over the organization of religious pilgrimages.[8] The ministry used the National Islamic Foundation (philanthropic religious foundations, or *waqfs*, are present in most Muslim countries) to sponsor research and publications on Islam. The government and council supported the foundation in the upkeep of mosques, libraries inside the mosques, and the training of imams. The training of imams was also accelerated until it reached 718,000 imans by 2010.[9]. The overall goal of the government and its agencies has been to utilize Islam as a nation-building device along with the Bengali language and culture. This goal was most prominently illustrated when the Islamic Foundation sponsored an encyclopedia of Islam in the Bengali language.[10]. Religion is the major difference between Islamic East Bengal (now Bangladesh) and Hindu West Bengal, areas which are otherwise indistinguishable in language and culture.

In 1984, the government intervened even more forcibly with the objective of tying Islam directly to the government by setting up a semi-official zakat system. Zakat is one of the pillars of Islam and requires believers to use a percentage of their income (at least 3 percent) for alms. This put government suasion beyond the voluntary contribution of charity. The funds raised from this directive were used to support orphanages, schools, children's hospitals, and charitable institutions and projects. [11] Beyond the direction of these funds, general funds are used to support other Muslim-related endeavors such as Islamic banks. The government does not persecute Hindus, Buddhists, and Christians. However, it does seek to align itself with Islam in part to build relations with other Islamic countries, especially the devout and wealthy Saudi Arabia. [12]

The most direct indicator of the role of Islam in Bangladesh is in the existence of religious parties and associations and their success on the national scene. The progenitor of all Islamic organizations and the initiator of the idea of carving a Muslim state out of India (which became both West Pakistan, now Pakistan, and East Pakistan, now Bangladesh) was the Muslim League. It was in fact established as a consequence of the partition of Bengal in 1905, which was favored by Muslims and opposed by Hindus. The rescinding of the partition in 1911 acted as an incentive for the Muslim League to represent Islamic interests. [13]

The League's continued advocacy of ongoing union with Pakistan in the late 1960s and early '70s made it almost inevitable that it would virtually disappear from the national stage after independence in 1971. It made a minor comeback in 1986 with four seats in parliament. Currently, its platform consists of opposition to the 51 percent hold that the government has in public industries such as utilities, transportation, and communications domestically, and reliance on India in foreign affairs. The party has since faded again. [14] Its successor was the Jamaat-e-Islam party. As was the case for the Muslim League, it faded for a while (in fact was prohibited) due to its anti-independence stance in 1971. It made a comeback in the 1980s as it became, for a time, the strongest opposition party. It adopted a hardline fundamentalist position. It opposed Western-style democracy and came out in favor of a democratic theocracy. It had the support of young madrassa students and others who advocated a return to traditional Islam. Although well-funded, it declined and only received 4.5 percent of votes in the 2008 election. [15]

A number of hardline Islamist parties have been on the scene for the past three decades. Most of these organizations advocate an Islamic state under sharia domestically and oppose India as a Hindu state internationally. The most radical of these associations is the Bangladesh Caliphate Movement, which wanted to establish a totally Islamic state. In addition, in line with its name, it called for a universal Islamic state or caliphate. As such, it did not oppose holy war or jihad in order to achieve its objectives. It also advocated the Qur'an and the Sunna as the bases for the operation of government. Another group, the Islamic United Front, was at the forefront of the opposition to the Treaty of Cooperation, Friendship, and Peace between Bangladesh and India. None of these groups have attained power. [16]

Private laws demonstrate greater Islamic influence. Bangladesh allows each religion a degree of latitude in private matters, including family issues. It does place limits on marriage between people of different religions as some other Muslim countries do. It does, however, have a Muslim Family Ordinance. This law incorporates some Islamic traditions. The statute affects inheritance (female relatives inherit less than male ones), marriage, and divorce. (In the last category, husbands have more divorce rights than wives). Societal custom in Bangladesh has always opposed polygamy, but this law allows the husband the right to have up to four wives as in the Qur'an.[17]

The preconditions for fundamentalist Islamism exist in Bangladesh. Corruption exists. An estimated 35 percent of people live below the poverty line, while underemployment reaches 40 percent. The country is so poor that its major export is people. It provides labor for Saudi Arabia, Oman, Qatar, Kuwait, the United Arab Emirates, and Malaysia.[18]

A glimmer of hope has appeared in the micro-credit program that gives small loans and credit to poor people, especially women in the rural areas. They receive assistance in producing crafts, small furniture, and even cellular phones in a program offered through the Grameen Bank under Muhammad Yunus. This program has stimulated cottage industries throughout rural Bangladesh. Gas discoveries on-shore and off-shore in Bangladesh are beginning to be exploited. Encouraging as these developments are, they are still only a small part of the economy.[19]Bangladesh remains an agricultural country whose main products of rice, jute, and tea are periodically devastated by cyclones wherein large-scale loss of property and life occur, as most of the country has an elevation of fifty feet or less, except for some hilly areas in the northeast and southeast. [20]

In spite of the above and Islam's importance in Bangladesh's society and life, Islam does not dominate the country. It has been used to build up national identity since independence. Bangladesh is a country with a distinct culture, language, and literature which goes back for centuries. It has also had a separate political status for centuries, the last few before the British raj as a Muslim-dominated Bengal.

The attempt of the government to identify with Islam over recent decades which culminated with the 1988 declaration of Islam as the state religion has not appreciably changed the political culture, which has alternated between military rule and the secular Awami League and the Bangladesh Nationalist parties. The legal system is based on English law, not sharia (although private domestic law, as previously indicated, does exhibit Islamic influence). Muslim participation in economic activities such as banking, evident in certain Islamic countries such as Indonesia, is not prominent as yet.[21]

Nevertheless, the heightened emphasis on Islam by the government may encourage the formation of Islamic parties and movements at both the local and national level. This may exacerbate conflict between the Muslim majority and the Hindu, Christian, Buddhist, and animist minorities. [22] On a political basis, it may also aggravate tensions between nonreligious secular parties and rising political fundamentalist parties. The establishment supports the first trend, government directives notwithstanding. The second trend may be supported by large numbers of students who graduate from madrassas and university students (including graduates of overseas institutions) looking for jobs who may seek radical change.

In the end, the Bangladesh establishment may be aided by two factors in combatting potential Islamic extremism. First, rural Bangladesh has a strong traditional/folk Islam basis. It is a society and culture where many women still practice *purdah*, or seclusion, and the culture is patriarchal as well as subject to pre-Islamic customs. The tradition of syncretism with Hinduism is also a barrier. Second, from the opposite direction, the forces of modernization and secularism, aided by rising literacy, especially among youth in the city, may also act as a barrier. Even though the rural population is gradually decreasing, the increasing growth of cities with an urbanization that looks forward, not backward, may provide compensation. It is too early to tell!

Concluding Comment: South Asia

The states of South Asia have to deal with cases of blurred identity. Azerbaijan is torn between Asia and Europe and the frontier between Christianity and Islam. It is located on the Caucasus turnstile between the Eurasian steppes and the Middle East. Both Afghanistan and Pakistan are concepts in which the constituent ethnic groups are the primary source of identity. Only Bangladesh has a sense of identity and is relatively homogenous, but it has sacrificed half of its patrimony, including a common culture, in the name of Islam. The area is a swirling kaleidoscope open to external forces.

General Conclusion

Certain common patterns are evident in the countries that are predominantly Muslim that have been studied in this work. First of all, Sufism has played a major if occasionally overlooked role in the culture and practice of Islam in Asia beyond the Middle East. As a practical guide to individual study, and through the prominent role played by Sufi brotherhoods, it has served as a bridge in various countries—a bridge between men and women, Shia and Sunni, pre-Islamic culture and Islam. The brotherhoods perform many essential social services in these countries. Second, although fundamentalism has arrived in various guises throughout these Islamic countries—Deobandism in Afghanistan and Pakistan, Wahhabiism in Azerbaijan and Uzbekistan, and Salafism in Turkmenistan and Indonesia, to illustrate several examples, individuals in these countries tend to follow the status quo Hanafi law code in these various states. Finally, each country has exhibited a certain amount of syncretism—whether it is adat, or customary law, in the Malay-speaking countries of Indonesia and Malaysia, preexisting Christianity in Azerbaijan, or Hindu and Buddhist beliefs in Bangladesh, all are intermingled with Islam to varying degrees in each country.

The Islamic countries studied in this work face similar problems. First, there are problems of identity. A number of these countries never existed until the past two decades. Nomadic societies such as Kazakhstan, Kyrgyzstan, and Turkmenistan never had centralized states within defined limits. Others such as Afghanistan and Pakistan are not based on a single ethnic group. Still others such as Malaysia have large groups that are not Malay-speakers. A number of these countries have equal or greater numbers outside of their defined borders, such as Azerbaijan, Tajikistan, and Uzbekistan, leading to strong irredentist feelings in these societies. In these cases, Islam has been used as a form of identity.

To one degree or another, these countries have been confronted by terrorism, whether homegrown as in Afghanistan, Indonesia, or Uzbekistan, or imported, such as in Tajikistan or Kyrgyzstan. Fundamentalism has arrived in all of these countries, but only in some has it transformed into violence. Nonetheless, all of these countries have faced the challenges which arrive with globalism, whether in the post-colonial states of Pakistan, Indonesia, Malaysia, and Bangladesh, or the post-Soviet states in the Caucasus and Central Asia. As a result,

Islam has been a two-edged sword for the governments of these countries. On the one hand, they proclaim their nationhood through secularism. On the other hand, the profession of Islam has been a tool of this nationalism and a link to other more developed Islamic countries in the Middle East. The question then becomes the role of Islam in cohabitation with a nation-state.

Other common problems confronting the countries under review revolve around economic pressures, political corruption, and environmental problems (such as desertification in Central Asia, or population density in Bangladesh and on the island of Java). How do countries handle high unemployment for the young as in Tajikistan, or the havoc caused by cyclones in Bangladesh, for example? Is Islam useful in these cases, or does it become a focus of discontent? How do countries which now have high literacy rates and increasing populations of young, educated but not fully employable people in still developing economies meet rising expectations? Does this become an issue for fundamentalist Islam? How do the authoritarian regimes in countries such as Azerbaijan and Uzbekistan satisfy people who may be attracted to membership in an idealized pan-Islamic state?

All of the Islamic states face these challenges in varying degrees, whatever their internal stage of development or civil society. Developing countries, such as Indonesia and Malaysia, as well as countries which still deal with poverty, such as Bangladesh and Pakistan, all struggle with the relationship between church and state. Countries undergoing external or internal strife, such as Azerbaijan or Afghanistan, respectively, or enjoying relative peace, such as Kazakhstan or Turkmenistan, still deal in some respect with the role of Islam. A force that represents one fifth of humanity cannot be ignored!

Endnotes

Endnotes: Indonesia

1. M. C. Ricklefs, *A History of Modern Indonesia since c. 1300*. London: MacMillan, 1991, pp. 3–13.

2. Azra Azyumardi, *The Origins of Islamic Reformism in Southeast Asia*. Honolulu: University of Hawaii Press, 2004, pp. 8–55.

3. Peter Riddell, *Islam and the Malay-Indonesian World*. Honolulu: University of Hawaii Press, pp. 70–78.

4. Ibid.

5. Ibid.

6. Ibid.

7. P. Jackson, "The Mystical Dimension," in *The Muslims of India: Beliefs and Practices*. Gujarat: The Anand Press, 1988, pp. 249–277.

8. B. A. Nicholson, *The Mystics of Islam*. London: Routledge & Kegan Paul, 1914a, 1963 (reprint), pp. 131, 139.

9. See Clifford Geertz, *The Religion of Java*. New York: The Free Press, 1960.

10. Geertz, *passim*.

11. Geertz, op. cit.

12. Ibid.

13. Consult, for example, Clifford Geertz, *The Social History of an Indonesian Town*. Cambridge: MIT Press, 2005.

14. Riddell, pp. 86–95.

15. Ibid.

16. Ibid., pp. 207–224.

17. Ricklefs, pp. 353–356. See also Bahtiar Effendy, *Islam and the State in Indonesia*. Athens: University of Ohio Press, 2003, pp. 131–134.

18. Ibid. (Effendy), pp. 31–32.

19. Ibid.

20. Ibid.

21. See a later section of the paper.

22. Effendy, pp. 7–38.

23. Ibid.

24. James J. Fox, "Currents in Contemporary Islam in Indonesia." *Harvard Asian Vision Paper*, 21, 2004, pp. 2–11.

25. Effendy, pp. 25–26.

26. "Tempo," 21–27 October and 18–24 November.

27. Riddell, pp. 287–322.

28. Ibid.

29. Ibid.

30. Ibid.

Endnotes: Malaysia

1. S. N. Eisenstadt, *Comparative Civilizations and Multiple Modernities*, Vol. 1 (Leiden: Brill, 2003), Chapter 36.
2. Ibid.
3. Robert Day McAmus, *Malay Muslims*,(Grand Rapids, Mich.: Wm. B. Erdmans, 2002), pp. 72–102.
4. Barbara Aoki Poisson, *The Growth and Influence of Islam* (Broomall, Pa.: Mason Crest, 2006), pp. 53–72.
5. http: //www.statistics.gov/my/, Department of Statistics, Malaysia.
6. See Raymond L. M. Lee and Susan E. Akerman, *Sacred Tensions* (Columbia, S.C.: University of South Carolina Press, 1997), pp. 16–27.
7. Ibid.
8. Michael G. Peletz, *Islamic Modern, Religious Courts and Cultural Politics in Malaysia* (Princeton: Princeton University Press, 2002), Chapter 2.
9. Ibid.
10. Ibid., Chapter 4.
11. Ibid. See also *USA Today*, February 17, 2010, Life section.
12. Poisson, pp. 74–75.
13. Ibid.
14. Ozay Mehmet, *Islamic Identity & Development* (Kuala Lampur: Forum, 1990), pp. 44–47.
15. See R. S. Milne and Diane K. Mauzy, *Malaysi: Tradition, Modernity, and Islam* (Boulder: Westview, 1986), pp. 126–151; Mehmet, pp. 47–48.
16. Mehmet, p. 48.
17. Ibid. See also John Miller and Aaron Kenedi, *Inside Islam* (New York: Marlowe & Company, 2002) for an overview.

Endnotes: Kazakhstan

1. See http://www:inform.kg?index.phys?lang+eng, the Kazakhstan Information Agency (accessed December 20, 2011).
2. Ibid.
3. Jim Corrigan, *The Growth and Influence of Islam in the Nations of Asia and Central Asia: Kazakhstan* (Broomall, Pa.: Mason Crest, 2005), pp. 35–86.
4. Ibid.
5. Ibid.
6. Alex Walters, "Islam in Kazakhstan: Modern and Moderate," http: //edgekz.com/almanac of Islam (accessed on December 22, 2011).
7. Corrigan, p. 38.
8. Ibid.
9. Ibid.

10.   Roberta Metcalf and Ingvar Svanberg, "Turkic Central Asia," in David Westerland and Ingvar Svanberg, eds., *Islam Outside the Arab World* (London: Curzon, 1999), pp. 149–165.

11.   T. Jeremy Gunn "Shaping an Islamic Identity," in *Sociology of Religion,* vol. 64, Issue 3, pp. 389–410.

12.   Ibid.

13.   Consult Cheryl Benard, "Central Asia: Apocalypse Now or Eclectic Surroundings," in the Rand McNally Corporation, *The Muslim World after 9/11,* pp. 321–366. See also http://www.rand.org/pubs/monographs/2006 (accessed December 23, 2011).

14.   Anna Zelkina, "Islam and Security in the New States of Central Asia: How Genuine Is the Islamic Threat?" in *Religion, State, and Society,* vol. 27, no. 374, pp. 360–387.

15.   Ahmed Rashad, *Jihad: The Rise of Militant Islam in Central Asia* (New York: Penguin Books, 2002), pp. 2–16.

16.   Reef Aloma, "The Influence of Islam in Post-Soviet Kazakhstan," in Beatrice F. Murray, ed., *Central Asia in Historical Perspective* (Boulder: Westview Press, 2005), pp. 164–180.

17.   See Library of Congress, "Kazakhstan Country Study," http://leweb 2.loc.gov/frd/ca/kztoc.html (accessed December 24, 2011).

18.   Walter, p. 2.

19.   Ibid.

20.   Corrigan, pp. 48–49.

21.   Rashad, pp. 200–215.

22.   Consult Oxford Islamic Studies Online, http://www.OxfordIslamicStudies.com/ap/t125/s/1247 (accessed December 24, 2011).

23.   Corrigan, pp. 63–68.

24.   Walters, pp. 2–3.

25.   Ibid.

Endnotes: Turkmenistan

1.   William M Habeeb, *The Growth and Influence of Islam in the Nations of Asia and Central Asia: Turkmenistan* (Philadelphia: Mason Crest Publishers, 2005), pp. 13–24.

2.   Ibid., pp. 24–36.

3.   See http:// www.Turkmens.com/Turkmenistan.html (accessed December 27, 2011).

4.   Scott Levi, "Turks and Tajiks in Central Asia," in *Everyday Life in Central Asia: Past and Present* (Bloomington: Indiana University Press, 2007), pp. 15–31.

5.   Consult Judy Bonavia et al., *The Silk Road* (Hong Kong: Odyssey Publications, 2004).

6.   Ahmed Rashid, *The Rise of Militant Islam in Central Asia* (New York: Penguin, 2002), pp. 19–22.

7.   Roustem Safronov, "Islam in Turkmenistan: the Niyazov Calculation," in Roald Sagdeev and Susan Eisenhower, eds., *Islam and Central Asia* (Washington, D.C.: Center for Political and Strategic Studies, 2000), pp. 74–76.

8.   Ibid.

9.   Rashid, pp. 7–15.

10.   Safronov, pp. 76–79.

11.   Consult http://www.eurasianet.org (accessed December 28, 2011).

12.   Ibid.

13.   Habeeb, p.85.

14.   Ibid., pp. 86–87.

15.   Consult Adrian Lynn Edgar, *Tribal Nation: The Making of Soviet Turkmenistan* (Princeton: Princeton University Press, 2004), *passim*.

16.   Habeeb, p. 87.

17.   Ibid., pp. 88–89.

18.   Ibid.

19.   Safronov, pp. 86–90.

20.   Ibid.

21.   Carole Blackwell, *Tradition and Society in Turkmenistan; Gender, Oral Culture, and Song* (London: Curzon Press, 2001) pp. 10–35.

22.   Kubicek, Paul 1998 "Authoritarianism in Central Asia: Curse or Cure?" *Third World Quarterly*, vol. 19, no. 1, pp. 29–43.

23.   Ibid.

Endnotes: Tajikistan

1.   Muriel Atkin. "Tajiks and the Persian World," in Beatrice F. Manz, ed., *Central Asia in Historical Perspective* (Boulder: Westview Press, 1994), pp. 127–143.

2.   BBC Country Profile: Tajikistan, http://news,BBC.com (accessed December 26, 2011).

3.   Colleen O'Dea, *The Growth and Influence of Islam in the Nations of Asia and Central Asia: Tajikistan* (Broomall, Pa.: Mason Crest, 2006), pp. 40–44.

4.   Saodat Olimova, "Islam and the Tajik Conflict," in Roald Sagdeev and Susan Eisenhower, eds., *Islam in Central Asia* (Washington, D.C.: Center for Political and Strategic Studies, 200), pp. 61–63.

5.   O'Dea, pp. 71–73, 99.

6.   Ahmed Rashid, *Jihad: The Rise of Militant Islam in Central Asia* (New York: Penguin Press, 2002), pp. 87–88.

7.   O'Dea, p. 53.

8.   Rashid, pp. 95–114.

9.   Ibid., pp. 43–45, 123ff.

10.   Olimova, p. 67.

11.   Rashid, pp. 106–114.

12.   Ibid.

13.   O'Dea, pp. 65–67.

14.   Emmanuel Karagiannis, "The Challenge of Radical Islam in Tajikistan: Hizb ut-Tahrir al-Islami," *Nationalities Papers*, vol. 34, issue 1, 2006, pp. 1–20.

15.   Rashid, pp. 137–158.

16.	Atkin, op.cit.

17.	See CIA World Factbook, 2011.

18.	Sebastien Peyrouse, "Islam in Central Asia: National Specificities and Postsoviet Globalisation,".*Religion, State and Society*, vol. 35, no. 3, 2007 pp. 245–260.

19.	Consult, for example, Michael Schwartz, "Islam's Rise..," *New York Times*, July 16, 2011.

20.	See http://www.eurasianet.org; also Consult http:// tajistan.tajnet.com./English/news.htm for background information.

Endnotes: Uzbekistan

1.	CIA Handbook 2011, http://www. cia.gov/cia/publications/factbook/geos/uz.html (accessed December 29, 2011).

2.	Joyce Libal, *The Growth and Influence of Islam in the Nations of Asia and Central Asia: Uzbekistan* (Broomall, Pa.: Mason Crest, 2005), pp. 13–15.

3.	Ibid., pp. 33–43.

4.	Martha Brill Olcott, "Islam in Uzbekistan," *Carnegie Paper* 91, July, 2008, pp. 2–8.

5.	Ibid.

6.	Ibid.

7.	Abdumannob Polab, "The Islamic Revival in in Uzbekistan," in Roald Sagdeev and Susan Eisenhower, eds., *Islam and Central Asia* (Washington, D.C.: Center for Political and Strategic Studies, 2000), pp. 53–5.

8.	Jessica N. Trisko, "Coping with the Islamist Threat: Analysing repression in Kazakhstan, Kyrgyzstan and Uzbekistan," *Central Asian Survey*, 24(4), pp. 373–389.

9.	Consult "Andijan Massacre Linked to Local Power Struggle," Eurasia website (http://www. eurasianet.org), September 28, 2005. (accessed January 2, 2012).

10.	See the Global Security Organization, military menu at http://www. global security/world/ html (accessed on January 3, 2012).

11.	United States Department of State (http://www.state.gov), Bureau of South and Central Asian Affairs, June 20, 2011: Uzbekistan (accessed January 2, 2012)._

12.	Ahmed Rashid, *Jihad: The Rise of Militant Islam in Central Asia* (New York: Penguin Books, 2002), Chapter 7, p. 137ff.

13.	Olivier Roy, *Islamic Resistance in Afghanistan* (Cambridge: Cambridge University Press, 1990), pp. 221–225.

14.	Rashid, pp. 137ff.

15.	Ibid., Chapters 7–8.

16.	Polat, pp. 39–51.

17.	Consult Olcutt, op. cit.

18.	Libal, p. 69.

19.	Ibid., p. 68.

20.	Rashid, pp. 126–127.

21.	Ibid.

22.	Libal, pp. 89–101.

Endnotes: Kyrgyzstan

1.   See "People and History: Kyrgyzstan," http://www.state.gov/r/pa/kygn/5755.htm (accessed January 3, 2012)
2.   Daniel E. Harmon, *The Growth and Influence of Islam in the Nations of Asia and Central Asia: Kyrgyzstan* (Philadelphia: Mason Crest, 2005), pp. 31–35.
3.   Ibid., pp. 36–41.
4.   Ibid., pp. 65–67.
5.   Anara Tabyshalieva, "The Kyrgyz and the Spiritual Dimensions of Daily Life," in Roald Sagdeev and Susan Eisenhower, eds., *Islam and Central Asia* (Washington, D.C.: The Center for Political and Strategic Studies, 2000), pp. 27–36.
6.   Ibid.
7.   See "Islam in Kyrgyzstan," http://islamawareness.net/Central Asia/Kyrgyzstan/iskyr.html.
8.   Consult http://www.cia.gov/cia/publications/factbook/geos/kg.html.
9.   Ahmed Rashid, *Jihad: The Rise of Militant Islam in Central Asia* (New York: Penguin Books, 2002), pp. 68–69.
10.   Islamic Awareness, op.cit.
11.   *World Almanac of Islamism*, http://www.almanac/afpc.org/Kyrgyzstan, p. 8.
12.   Ibid.
13.   Ibid.
14.   Tabyshalieva, pp. 32–37.
15.   Rashid, pp. 153, 160 –173.
16.   World Almanac of Islam, op.cit., pp. 4–8.
17.   Ibid.
18.   Ibid.
19.   Tabyshalieva, pp. 28–29.
20.   Ibid.
21.   Ibid., pp. 32–33.
22.   Ibid. p. 34.
23.   Ibid.
24.   Ibid., pp. 35–37; see also http://eng.gateway.kg.
25.   Glenn Curtis, ed., *Kyrgyzstan: A Country Study* (Washington, D.C.: GPO, n.d.) n.p. available; also at http://country studies.US/Kyrgyzstan (accessed January 4, 2012).
26.   Tabyshalieva, pp. 28–9ff. Also consult Jeff Sahadeo and Russell Zanca, eds., *Everyday Life in Central Asia* (Bloomington: Indiana University Press, 2007), *passim*.

Endnotes: Afghanistan

1.   See Department of State, Bureau of Public Affairs, Bureau of South and Central Asia, "Afghanistan."
2.   Olivier Roy, *Islam and Resistance in Afghanistan* (Cambridge: Cambridge University Press, 1990), pp. 38–43.

3.   Ibid., pp. 44–50.

4.   Ibid., pp. 38–43.

5.   Ibid., pp. 53–65.

6.   Consult http://www.global security.org/military/intro/islam-deobandi.htm.

7.   F. Rahman, *Revival and Reform in Islam: A Study of Islamic Fundamentalism* (Oxford: Oxford University Press, 2000), p. 168.

8.   Roy, pp. 70–71.

9.   Ibid., pp. 110–118.

10.   Kristin Mendoza, *Islam and Islamism in Afghanistan,* History Project, Harvard School of Law, http://www.law.harvard.edu/programs/ilsp/research/mendoza.pdf.

11.   Ibid.

12.   Ahmed Rashid, *Taliban: Militant Islam, Oil, and Fundamentalism in Central Asia* (New Haven: Yale University Press, 2007), p. 26.

13.   Mendoza, pp. 2, 7 –12. Also consult Jon Anderson, "How Afghans Define Themselves in Relation to Islam," in M. Nazif Shahrami and Robert L. Canfield, eds., *Revolution and Rebellion in Afghanistan* (Berkeley: University of California Press, 1987), p. 274.

14.   Ahmed Rashid, "Islam in Central Asia: Afghanistan and Pakistan," in Roald Sagdeev and Susan Eisenhower, eds., *Islam and Central Asia* (Washington, D.C.: Center for Political and Strategic Studies, 2000), pp. 225–240.

15.   Roy, p. 30.

16.   Ibid., pp. 31–32.

17.   Ibid., pp. 33–38.

18.   A. Olesen, *Islam and Politics in Afghanistan* (Richmond: Curzon Press, 1995), pp. 96–99.

19.   Rashid, pp. 241–266.

20.   Olivier Roy, "Has Islamism a Future in Afghanistan?" in William Maley, ed., *Fundamentalism Reborn: Afghanistan and the Rise of the Taliban* (New York: New York University Press, 1998), pp. 206–210.

Endnotes: Azerbaijan

1.   Gerald Robbins, *The Growth and Influence of Islam in the Nations of Asia and Central Asia* (Philadelphia: Mason Crest Publishers, 2005), pp. 13–19.

2.   Ibid., pp. 27–31.

3.   Ibid., pp. 31–34.

4.   Ibid., p. 118.

5.   See CIA, *The World Factbook*, http://www.cia.gov/cia/publications/factbook/geos/aj.html .

6.   Anar Valiyev, "Azerbaijan: Islam in a Post-Soviet Republic," *Middle East Review of International Affairs,* vol. 9, no.4, December 22, 2005, p.1.

7.   Ibid., p.7.

8.   Ibid., p. 8.

9.   Raul Monika, "Islam in Post-Soviet Azerbaijan," in *Archives des Sciences Social des Religions,* vol.115 (Summer 2001), p. 113.

10. Alec Rasizade, "Azerbaijan in Transition in the New Age of Democracy," *Communist and Post-Communist Studies,* vol. 36, no. 3 (2003), pp. 342–343.

11. Robbins, pp. 55–57.

12. Ibid., pp. 53–55, 85–87.

13. Ibid., p. 97.

14. Arif Yusuvov, *Islam in Azerbaijan*(Baku: Zamani Press, 2004), *passim.*

15. Svant Cornell, *Politicization of Islam,* http://www.silkwood studies/org/view/docs/silkroad papers/0610.Azei/pdf, p. 23 (accessed January 4, 2012).

16. See http://azerb.com.

17. Valiyev, p. 6.

18. Ibid., pp. 7–11.

19. See H. Kotecka,"Islamic and Ethnic Identities in Azerbaijan: Emerging Trends and Tensions: A Discussion Paper" (2006), http://www. osce.org/Baku/238094 (accessed January 5, 2012).

20. Ibid.

21. Robbins, pp. 74–75.

22. Consult http://www.bakusun.az:8101/index.html.

23. Ibid.

24. Robbins, pp. 83–84.

25. Ibid.

Endnotes: Pakistan

1. D. P. Singhal, *Indian and World Civilization* (Calcutta: Rupa & Co, 1972), Chapter IV.

2. Clarissa Aykroyd, *The Growth and Influence of Islam in the Nations of Asia and Central Asia Pakistan* (Broomall, Pa.: Mason Crest Publishers, 2005), pp. 42–47.

3. The role of Islam in Pakistan vis-à-vis the secular state was debated even before the state was founded. See, for example, Asad Ahmed, "Advocating a Secular Pakistan: The Munir Report of 1954," in Barbara D. Metcalf, ed., *Islam in South Asia* (Princeton: Princeton University Press, 2009), Chapter 32.

4. Aykroyd, p. 54.

5. Mumtaz Mahal, "Parliament, Polls, and Islam," in *American Journal of Islamic Social Sciences,* 1/2/1985, pp. 115–128.

6. See CIA World Factbook, "Pakistan," http://www.cia.gov/cia/publications/factbook/geos/pk.html.

7. Consult Library of Congress, "Country Profiles: Pakistan," at http://lcweb.2.doc.gov/frd/cs/profiles/Pakistan.

8. The Pakistan Virtual Library has a collection of articles on Pakistan, http://www.clas.ufl.edu/users/hthursby/pak/index.htm.

9. Ahmed Rashid, "Islam in Central Asia: Afghanistan and Pakistan", in Roald Sagdeev and Susan Eisenhower, eds., *Islam and Central Asia* (Washington, D.C.: Central for Political and Strategic Studies, 2000), pp. 221–227.

10. Farooq Qaiser Gondal, "US Drone Attacks in Pakistan," in *Washington Times Online*, November 20, 2011 (Sunday Edition).

11. Rashid, pp. 230–237.

12. Ibid.

13. Frederic Grare, *Political Islam in the Indian Sub-Continent* (New Delhi: Monohar Press, 2002), pp. 11–13.

14. Ackroyd, pp. 54–58.

15. Grare, pp. 11–13, *passim.*

16. Martin Lewis, "Deobandi Islam vs. Barelvi Islam," Geo Currents, http://geocurrents.info/cultural-geography/deobandi-Islam-vs_barelvi-Islam-in_south-asia (accessed January 10, 2012).

17. Ibid.

18. Rashid, p. 231.

19. Lewis, op. cit.

20. Ibid.

21. See "Muslims Unite Against the Taliban," no author listed, in *The Washington Times,* May 25, 2009, http://www.WashingtonTimes.com/news/2009/mag/12/muslim-leaders-unite-against-the-Taliban.

22. Consult http://www.infopak.gov.pk/ for sources on current stories and details on the orders.

23. Aykroyd, p. 82.

24. Library of Congress, "Pakistan," op.cit.

Endnotes: Bangladesh

1. Doris Valliant, *The Growth and Influence of Islam in the Nations of Asia and Central Asia: Bangladesh* (Philadelphia: Mason Crest, 2005), pp. 30–50.

2. Ibid., pp. 67–84.

3. Islam Md. Rafiqul, "Islam in Bangladeshi Society," *SACS*, vol. 2, no. 2, p. 5.

4. L. Ziriq, *Bangladesh: From Mujib to Ershad: An Interpretative Study* (Karachi and New York: Oxford University Press, 1995), pp. 254–260.

5. Rafiqul, pp. 4–6.

6. P.J. Bertocci, *The Politics of Community and Culture in Bangladesh* (Dhaka: Center for Social Studies, 1996), p. 138.

7. Rafiqul, pp. 7–8.

8. See "Islamism and the State," *World Almanac of Islam*, July 14, 2011, http://almanac.afpc.org/Bangladesh.

9. Rafiqul, p. 8.

10. Consult Sufi M. Uddin, *Constructing Bangladesh: Religion, Ethnicity, and Language in an Islamic Nation* (Chapel Hill: University of North Carolina Press, 2005), pp. 54–56 *passim*.

11. Ibid.

12. World Almanac of Islam, op.cit.

13. See James Heitzman et al., eds., *Bangladesh: A Country Study* (Washington, D.C.: GPO, 1989) n.p. for the chapter on the division of Bengal.

14. Consult http:// Bangladesh.com/politicalparties for a contemporary description of political parties.

15. The website http:// www. Jamaal-i-Islami.org/index.php?option.com__archive 8 is put out by one of the major parties.

16. Sunita Paul, "Bangladesh: They Hate the US and the West Here Too," in *Global Politics-South Asia*, March 30, 2008.

17. Rafiqul, p. 9.

18. Valliant, pp. 51–52.

19. Ibid. pp. 56–58.

20. Ibid. pp. 20, 52–53.

21. Bangladesh.com, op.cit.

22. The CIA World Factbook has relevant information on Bangladesh, particularly the sections "Government" and "Society," http:// www.cia.gov/cia/publicqations/factbook/geos/bg.html.

Select Bibliography of Books or Articles Used or Consulted

Indonesia

Azyumardi, Azra (2004). *The Origins of Islamic Reformism in Southeast Asia.* Honolulu: University of Hawaii Press.

Effendy, Bahtiar (2002). *Islam and the State in Indonesia.* Athens: University of Ohio Press.

Fox, James (2004). "Currents in Contemporary Islam in Indonesia." *Harvard Asian Vision Paper* (21: 2–11).

Geertz, Clifford (1960). *The Religion of Java.* New York: The Free Press.

Geertz, Clifford (2005). *The Social History of an Indonesian Town.* Cambridge: MIT Press.

Jackson, P. (1988). "The Mystical Dimension," in P. Jackson, ed., *The Muslims of India: Beliefs and Practices.* Gujerat: The Anand Press.

Mehmet, Ozay (1990). *Islamic Identity and Development.* Kuala Lampur: Forum.

Nicholson, B.A. (1914, 1963 reprint). *The Mystics of Islam.* London: Routledge & Kegan Paul.

Ricklefs, M. C.(1991). *A History of Modern Indonesia since c. 1300.* London: Macmillan.

Riddell, Peter (2006). *Islam and the Malay-Indonesian World.* Honolulu: University of Hawaii Press.

Malaysia

Azyumardi, Azra (2004). *The Origins of Islamic Reformism in Southeast Asia.* Honolulu: University of Hawaii Press.

Eisenstadt, S. N. (2003). *Comparative Civilizations and Multiple Modernities.* Leiden: Brill

Lee, Raymond I. M. and Susan F. Akerman (1997). *Sacred Tensions.* Columbia, S.C.: University of South Carolina Press.

McAmus, Robert Day (2002). *Muslims.* Grand Rapids, Mich.: Wm B. Erdmans.

Mehmet, Ozay (1990). *Islamic Identity and Development.* Kuala Lampur: Forum.

Miller, John and Aaron Kenedi (2002). *Inside Islam.* New York: Marlowe & Company.

Milne, R. S. and Diane K. Mauzy (1986). *Malaysia: Tradition, Modernity, and Islam.* Boulder, Colo.: Westview Press.

Peletz, Michael G. (2002). *Islamic Modern, Religious Courts and Cultural Politics in Malaysia.* Princeton: Princeton University Press.

Poisson, Barbara Aoki (2006). *The Growth and Influence of Islam in Asia and Central Asia: Malaysia.* Broomall, Pa.: Mason Crest.

Riddell, Peter (2006). *Islam and the Malay-Indonesian World.* Honolulu: University of Hawaii Press.

Kazakhstan

Aloma,Reef (2005). "The Influence of Islam in Post-Soviet Kazakhstan," in Beatrice F. Murray, ed., *Central Asia in Historical Perspective*. Boulder: Westview.

Benard, Cheryl (2011). "Central Asia: Apocalypse Now or Eclectic Surroundings," in Rand McNally Corporation, *The Muslim World after 9/11*. New York: Rand McNally.

Corrigan, Jim (2005). *The Growth and Influence of Islam in the Nations of Asia and Central Asia: Kazakhstan.* Broomall, Pa.: Mason Crest.

Gunn, Jeremy (2010). "Shaping an Islamic Identity," in *Sociology of Religion*, vol. 64, issue 3, pp. 389–410.

Metcalf, Roberta and Ingvar Svanberg (1999). "Turkic Central Asia," in David Westerland and Ingvar Svanberg, eds., *Islam Outside the Arab World*. London: Curzon.

Murray, Beatrice F., ed.(2005). *Central Asia in Historical Perspective*. Boulder: Westview.

Rashad, Ahmed (2002). *Jihad: The Rise of Militant Islam in Central Asia.* New York: Penguin.

Walters, Alex (2011). "Islam in Kazakhstan: Modern and Moderate." http: //edgekz.com.

Almanac of Islam (accessed December 22, 2011).

Westerland, David and Ingvar Svanberg, eds.(1999). *Islam Outside the Arab World*. London: Curzon.

Zelkina, Anna (2005). "Islam and Security in the New States of Central Asia," in *Religion, State, and Society*, vol. 27, no. 374, pp. 360–387.

Turkmenistan

Blackwell, Carole (2001). *Tradition and Society in Turkmenistan: Gender, Oral Culture, and Song.* London: Curzon.

Bonavia, Judy et al. (2004). *The Silk Road*. Hong Kong: Odyssey Publications.

Edgar, A. L. (2004). *Tribal Nation: The Making of Soviet Turkmenistan.* Princeton: Princeton University Press.

Habeeb, William M. (2005). *The Growth and Influence of Islam in the Nations of Asia and Central Asia: Turkmenistan.* Philadelphia: Mason Crest Publishers.

Kubicek, Paul (1998). "Authoritarianism in Central Asia: Curse or Cure?" *Third World Quarterly*, vol. 19, no. 1, pp. 29–43.

Levi, Scott (2007). "Turks and Tajiks," in Jeff and Russell Zanca, eds., *Everyday Life in Central Asia*. Bloomington: Indiana University Press.

Rashad, Ahmad. *The Rise of Militant Islam in Central Asia.* New York: Penguin.

Safronov, Roustem (2000). "Islam in Turkmenistan: the Niyazov Calculation," in Roald Sagdeevand Susan Eisenhower, eds., *Islam and Central Asia*. Washington, D.C.: Center for Political and Strategic Studies.

Sagdeev, Roald and Susan Eisenhower, eds. (2000). *Islam and Central Asia*. Washington, D.C.: Center for Political and Strategic Studies.

Zelkina, Anna (2008). "Islam and Security in the New States of Central States: How Genuine Is the Islamic Threat?" in *Religion, State, and Society*, vol. 27, no. 374, pp. 360–384.

Tajikistan

Atkin, Muriel (1999). "Tajiks and the Persian World," in Beatrice F. Manz, ed., *Central Asia in Historical Perspective*. Westview Press, 1994.

Karagiannis, Emmanuel (2006). "The Challenge of Radical Islam in Tajikistan: Hizb ut-Tahrir-al-Islami," *Nationalities Papers,* vol. 34, issue 1, pp. 1–20.

Kubicek, Paul. See Turkmenistan bibliography.

Levi, Scott. See Turkmenistan bibliography.

O'Dea, Colleen (2006). *The Growth and Influence of Islam in the Nations of Asia nd Central Asia: Tajikistan.* Broomall, Pa.: Mason Crest.

Olinova, Saodat(2000). "Islam and the Tajik Conflict" in Sagdeev and Eisenhower (see Bibliography of Turkmenistan for full citation,), pp. 60–*passim*.

Peyrouse, Sebastien (2007). " Islam in Central Asia: National Specificities and Post-Soviet Globalisation," in *Religion, State, and Society,* vol. 35, no. 3, pp. 2007.

Rashad, Ahmed. See Kazakhstan bibliography.

Safronov, Roustem. See Turkmenistan bibliography.

Schwartz, Michael (2011). "Islam's Rise...," *New York Times,* July 16.

Uzbekistan

Benard, Cheryl. See Kazakhstan bibliography.

Kubicek, Paul. See Turkmenistan bibliography.

Levi, Scott. See Turkmenistan bibliography .

Libal, Joyce (2005). *The Growth and Influence of Islam in the Nations of Asia and Central Asia: Uzbekistan.* Broomall, Pa.: Mason Crest.

Metcalf, Roberta. See Kazakhstan bibliography.

Olcott, Martha Brill (2008). "Islam in Uzbekistan," *Carnegie Paper*, 91, July, 2008.

Polab, Abdumannob (2000). "The Islamic Revival in Uzbekistan," in Sagdeev and Eisenhower, pp. 53–55; see Turkmenistan bibliography for full citation.

Rashid, Ahmed. See Kazakhstan bibliography.

Roy, Olivier (1990). *Islamic Resistance in Afghanistan*. Cambridge: Cambridge University Press.

Trisko, Jessica N. (2009). "Coping with the Islamist Threat: analyzing repression in Kazakhstan, Kyrgyzstan and Uzbekistan," *Central Asian Survey*, 24 (4), pp. 373–389.

Kyrgyzstan

Curtis, Glenn, ed. (2012). *Kyrgyzstan: A Country Study*. Washington, D.C.: GPO.

Gunn, T. Jeremy. See Kazakhstan bibliography.

Harmon, Daniel E. (2005). *The Growth and Influence of Islam in the Nations of Asia and Central Asia:Kyrgyzstan*. Philadelphia: Mason Crest.

Kubicek, Paul. See Turkmenistan bibliography.

Levi, Scott. See Turkmenistan bibliography.

Rashid, Ahmed. See Kazakhstan bibliography.

Sagdeev, Roald, and Susan Eisenhower. See Turkmenistan bibliography.

Sahedeo, Jeff and Russell Zanca, eds. (2007). *Everyday Life in Central Asia*. Bloomington: Indiana University Press.

Tabyshalieva, Anara (2000). "The Kyrgyz and the Spiritual Dimensions of Daily Life," pp. 27–36, in Sagdeev and Eisenhower.

Trisko, Joyce. See Uzbekistan bibliography.

Afghanistan

Anderson, Jon (1987). "How Afghans Define Themselves in Relation to Islam," M. Nazif Shahrami and Robert L. Canfield, eds., in *Revolution and Rebellion in Afghanistan*, Berkeley: University of California Press.

Maley, William, ed. (1998). *Fundamentalism Reborn: Afghanistan and the Rise of the Taliban*. New York: New York University Press.

Mendoza, Kristin (2010). *Islam and Islamism in Afghanistan*. History Project, Harvard School of Law.

Nazif, Shahrami and Robert L. Canfield, eds. (1987). *Revolution and Rebellion in Afghanistan* Berkeley: University of California Press.

Oleson, A. (1995). *Islam and Politics in Afghanistan.* Richmond: Curzon Press.

Rahman, F. (2000). *Revival and Reform in Islam: A Study of Islamic Fundamentalism.* Oxford: Oxford University Press.

Rashid, Ahmed (2000). "Islam in Central Asia: Afghanistan and Pakistan," in Sagdeev and Eisenhower, eds. *Islam and Central Asia*, pp. 225–266; see Turkmenistan bibliography.

Rashid, Ahmed (2007). *Taliban: Militant Islam, Oil, and Fundamentalism in Central Asia.* New Haven: Yale University Press.

Roy, Olivier (1990). See Uzbekistan bibliography.

Roy, Olivier (1998). "Has Islamism a Future in Afghanistan?" in Maley (see above), pp. 206–210.

Azerbaijan

Cornell, Svant (2012). *Politicization of Islam.* http://www.silkwood, accessed January 4, 2012.

Kotecka, H. (2006). "Islamic and Ethnic Identities in Azerbaijan: Emerging Trends and Tensions—A Discussion Paper." http://www.osce.org/Baku/238094.

Monika, Raul (2001). "Islam in Post-Soviet Azerbaijan," in *Archives des Sciences Social des Religions*, vol.115 (Summer 2001).

Nicholson, B. A. See Indonesia bibliography.

Rahman, F. See Afghanistan bibliography .

Rasizade, Alec (2003). "Azerbaijan in Transition in the New Age of Democracy," *Communist and Post-Communist Studies,* vol. 36, no. 3, pp. 342–346.

Robbins, Gerald (2005). *The Growth and Influence of Islam in Asia and Central Asia: Azerbaijan.* Philadelphia: Mason Crest Publishers.

Valiyev, Anar (2005). "Azerbaijan: Islam in a Post-Soviet Republic," *Middle East Review of International Affairs,* vol. 9, no. 4.

Westerland, David (1999). See Kazakhstan bibliography.

Yusouvov, Arif (2004). *Islam in Azerbaijan.* Baku: Zamani Press.

Pakistan

Ahmed, Asad (2009). "Advocating a Secular Pakistan: The Munir Report of 1954," in Barbara D. Metcalf, ed., *Islam in South Asia.* Princeton: Princeton University Press.

Aykroyd, Clarissa (2005). *The Growth and Influence of Islam in the Nations of Asia and Central Asia: Pakistan.* Broomall, Pa.: Mason Crest Publishers.

Gondal, Farooq Quaiser (2011). "US Drone Attacks in Pakistan," in *Washington Times Online*, November 20, 2011 (Sunday edition).

Grare, Frederic (2002). *Political Islam in the Indian Sub-Continent*. New Delhi: Monohar Press.

Lewis, Martin (2012). "Deobandi Islam vs Barelvi Islam," Geo Currents, http://geocurrents.info/cultural, accessed on January 10, 2012.

Mahal, Mumtaz (1985). "Parliaments, Polls, and Islam," in *American Journal of Islamic Social Sciences*, 1/2, pp. 115–128.

Metcalf, Barbara D., ed. (2009). *Islam in South Asia*. Princeton: Princeton University Press.

Rahman, F. See Afghanistan bibliography.

Rashid, Ahmed. "Islam in Central Asia: Afghanistan and Pakistan." See Afghanistan bibliography.

Singhal, D. P. (1972). *Indian and World Civilization*. Calcutta: Rupa &Co.

Bangladesh

Bertocci, P. J.(1996). *The Politics of Community and Culture in Bangladesh*. Dhaka: Center for Social Studies.

Heitzman, James et al., eds. (1989). *Bangladesh: A Country Study*. Washington, D.C.: GPO.

Lee, Raymond and Susan E. Akerman, 1997. See Malaysia bibliography .

Mehmet, Ozay (1990). See Malaysia bibliography.

Paul, Sunita (2008). "Bangladesh: They Hate the US and the West Here Too," in *Global Politics-South Asia*, March 30, 2008.

Rafiqul, Islam Md. "Islam in Bangladeshi Society," *SACS*, vol 2, no. 2.

Singhal, D. P. See Pakistan bibliography.

Uddin, Sufi M. (2005). *Constructing Bangladesh: Religion, Ethnicity, and Language in an Islamic Nation*. Chapel Hill: University of North Carolina Press.

Valliant, Doris (2005). *The Growth and Influence of Islam in the Nations of Asia and Central Asia and Central Asia: Bangladesh*. Philadelphia: Mason Crest.

Ziriq, L. (1995). *From Mujib to Ershad*. New York: Oxford University Press.

Glossary

Glossary for chapter on Indonesia

Abangan--an example of syncretism in Java that combines indigenous beliefs, Buddhism, and Hinduism with Islamic practices.

Aceh--stronghold for Islamic beliefs in north Sumatra.

Bali--Hindu outpost in Muslim Indonesia.

Dkir--Sufi practices that involves the repeated recitation of the name of God in mediation services.

Istiqama--principle of integrity of faith invoked in Indonesia/

Jam'ah Islamiya--radical Muslim group which seeks to unite all Muslims in Southeast Asia.

Java--most populous island in Indonesia.

Kalimantan-- current name for Borneo shared by Indonesia and Malaysia.

Kebatim-- combination of animism, Buddhism, Hinduism, and Islam granted official recognition in Indonesia.

Lasyk Jihad--ilitant Islamic organization (now disbanded) which fought Christians in Maluku and Sulawesi in communal battles.

Muhammadiya--modernist Islamic organization which runs schools, hospitals, and other social institutions throughout Indonesia.

Nahdlatul Ulama--traditional Muslim organization which runs schools, hospitals, and other social institutions throughout Indonesia.

Pancasilla--an acronym for nationalism, humanism, democracy, social welfare, and belief in God.

Santri--pious observant Muslims resident mostly in Java who send their children to mostly rural Islamic schools.

Sufi--devotional mystical version of Islam that emphasized individual meditation.

Sulawesi--current name for Celebes.

Sumatra-- second most populous island in Indonesia.

Wali--Islamic saint)s) followed by Sufi adherents.

West Arian--Indonesian name for their portion of New Guinea.

Zakat--giving of alms which is of the Five Pillars of Islam.

Glossary for chapter on Malaysia-

ABIM--Acronym for the Malaysia Islamic Youth Movement dominant on university compuses.

Adat--traditional pre-Islamic customs.

Anwar Ibrahim—head of Muslim youth groups who was deputy Prime Minister before he was removed.

Bumaputra--definition for Malay and other "original inhabitants of Malaysia" who must be Muslims to qualify for government preferential treatment.

Dakwah--term for fundamentalist organizations that seek to convert non-Muslims.

East Borneo-- non-peninsular Malaysia.

Haditha--sayings of the Prophet.

Islamic Party of Malaysia--sectarian opposition party.

Jemant Tablegh--prominent Dakwah organization active in both rural and urban areas.

Melakah-- current name for Malacca original entry point for Islam.

Muhammad Mehangir--former authoritarian leader of the country.

National Front Alliance--governing coalition in Malaysia.

PERKIM-- acronym for Islamic Welfare and Missionary Association which is active in schools and other social organizations.

Sabah--new name for the Malaysian part of Borneo (North Borneo and Sarawak) formerly East Borneo.

Sisters in Islam--progressive women's Muslim movement.

Straits of Malacca--strategic waterway that is a link between the Indian and Pacific Oceans and an historical choke point and entry way for trade and missionary activity.

Ulama/ulema--Muslim scholars.

Umma--global Islamic religious/legal/political community.

Glossary for chapter on Kazakhstan

Caspian Sea--large body of water which borders Central Asia.

Chingish Khan (also Genghis Khan)--Mongol conqueror who established rule over Central Asia.

Great Silk Road--historical trading route (actually a number of routes) which connected China with Europe and ran through Central Asia.

Hajj--religious pilgrimage to Mecca.

Halah--purified meat for Muslims.

Hanafi--religious law code followed by most Sunni Muslims in Asia.

Hijab--veil worn by Muslim women

Great Horde--multi-ethnic mass of invaders led by Mongols which swept through many parts of the globe which also refers to one of the three main confederations among Kazakhs.

Little Horde--another confederation among the Kazakhs.

Kazakhs--the major ethnic group within the country,

Middle Horde--the third of the major Kazakh tribal confederations.

Mongols--the invaders who brought the Kazakhs in their wake.

Nazarbayev- -Nursultan Nazarbayev has led the country since 1990.

Tatars—the name for the Turkic-speakers who occupied Central Asia in the middle of the first millennium C.E.

Turkic speakers—the language family for most of Central Asia.

Talas—battle near southern Kazakhstan in which the Arabs defeated the Chinese which led to the introduction of Islam into Central Asia.

Zhuzes—The Kazakh word for hordes or clans.

Glossary for chapter on Turkmenistan

Allah--the supreme deity in Islam and the Muslim term for God.

Basmachi Rebellion--Islamic-based rebellion against Russian/Soviet rule between 1916 and 1920.

Bukhara--Uzbek Khanate which dominated part of northern Turkistan before Russian rule.

Council of Religious Affairs--supervises all religious affairs in the country.

Gengish--Turkmen term for the above.

Khiva--econd Uzbek Khanate which vied for power in the northern part of the country before the Russian period.

Mecca--Islamic holy city.

Merv--founded in the sixth century BCE, this city was a thriving trading cnter on the Great Silk Road and the capital of the Seljuk Empire from the 10th through 12th centuries.

Mosques--Islamic centers of worship.

Niyazov--President of the country until 2006.

Oghuz--Branch of the Turks who founded both the Seljuk and Ottoman Empirew.

Parthians--Persian rulers from 200 BCE to 200CE.

Rukhnama--spiritual guide compared to the Bible or Qur'an published by the president which was at one time required reading in every school.

Sassanians--Persian rulers between 200 and 600 C.E.

Seleucids--Greek rulers from 330 to 200 BCE.

Tengri--traditional deity conflated with Allah.

Turkmenbashi Ruhe--largest mosque in Central Asia.

Turkmenchalik--eponymous ancestor of the Turkmen.

Glossary for chapter on Tajikistan

Badakshan--separatist area in Tajikistan mainly populated by non-Tajiks.

Deobandi--fundamentalist Islamic movement centered from seminaries in Pakistan.

Ferghana Valley--most fertile area in Central Asia which abuts three countries and is a center of Islamic ferment.

Hizb-ut-Tehir--Islamic fundamentalist movement active in Central Asia which promotes a universal Islamic state.

Islamic Movement of Turkistan--radical Muslim movement which is an offshoot of the the Islamic Movement of Uzbekistan and is often violent in its methods.

Islamic Movement of Uzbekistan--the major radical extremist Muslim organization in Central Asia which has been involved in military conflict in Uzbekistan and Kyrgyzstan as well as Tajikistan.

Islamic Renaissance Party--the only officially recognized Islamic opposition party in Central Asia.

Karategen Valley--another separatist area.

Nestorian--Pre-Islamic Christian group which still has a few adherents.

Pamirs, Pamiri-- mountain ranges which is the home of the non-Takij Pamiri.

Qur'an--Muslim Holy Book

Rahmonov--President since 1992

Tajiks--only major group in Central Asia that speaks a non-Turkic language. The Iranian-speaking Tajiks have about half of their people living in Afghanistan and Uzbekistan.

Wahhabis--fundamentalist sect from Saudi Arabia

Zorastrianism--Persian derived religion which pre-dates Islam.

Glossary for Chapter on Uzbekistan

Andijan Massacre-- a large scale killing of protestors who were protesting against economic conditions in 2005.

Council of Religious Affairs--supervisory board for religious matters in Uzbekistan.

ERK--also known as the Freedom Party; it is the main opposition movement.

Islam Karamov--authoritarian ruler since 1990

Jadidism--reform Islamic movement that arose among educated Muslims of the upper and middle classes early in the twentieth century.

Kokand--historic city and khanate along the Great Silk Road.

Mahallas--local committees that oversee both traditional and Islamic activities/

Nursi movement--movement imported from Turkey which mingles religious teaching with science.

Posbon--government official who now supervises each mahalla.

Samarkand--fabled city (and one of the oldest in the world) which Timur made his capital.

Samizdat--nderground press which existed in Uzbekistan as well as Russia during the last years of the Soviet regime.

Tarika--Muslim brotherhoods active in Uzbekistan.

Tashkent--the capital with both historical significance and contemporary significance as the home of the largest university in Central Asia and a modern industrial metropolis.

Uzbeks--the largest ethnic group in Central Asia with over 20 million in the country and several million outside its borders.

Glossary for chapter on Kyrgyzstan

Bishkek--capital of Kyrgyzstan.

Chu Valley--northern section of the country where a more secular tradition prevails

Dungees--a minority group located in the Ferghana valley,

East Turkistan Islamic Party—Islamic party outlawed in 2003.

Kurban ait -- traditional holiday celebrated on June 10.

Jalal-Abad--- third largest city located in the Ferghana valley and a center of Islamic learning.

Kyrgyz--the majority group in the country with some affinity to the Kazakhs.

Islamic Party of Turkistan -- offshoot of Islamic Movement of Uzbekistan.

Manchu--Chinese dynasty which dominated northern and eastern Kyrgyzstan before the arrival of the Russians/

Mazar-- religious shrines located throughout the country,

Oroz Ait--feast day at the end of Ramadan which combines Muslim and Turkic customs.

Osh--second largest city of ancient origins which has a Muslim university and over 50 mosques.

Ramadan--the 9th month of the Muslim lunar year where people fast from dawn to dusk in compliance with the fourth pillar of Islam.

Samk--organization which supervises Islamic activities within the country.

Shamanism--the practice of following traditional holy men.

Turkish Liberation Organization--a radical fundamentalist organization.

Glossary for chapter on Afghanistan

Alim--local religious figure.

Chisthtiyya--Sufi order especially strong in the Sub-continenet.

Fiqh--the interpretation of Islamic law.

Guardians of the Revolution--radical Iranian –backed grouping among the Shia/.

Haqqani Network--extremist Muslim group recently branded as extremist.

Hazara--persecuted group descended from Mongols mostly Shia.

Harakat-i-inquilab-islami--moderate clerical political grouping among the Sunni.

Heckmatyar—anti-western leader active in Aghan politics since the 1960's.

Hizb-i-Islami--A political grouping identified with Heckmatyr now split into two factions—the original branch and a more moderate offshoot.

Jamiyat-e-Islami--moderate Sunni movement supported by people from the north and the naqsha-bandiyya Sufi Order

Karzai-- leader of Afghanistan since 2002

Khalis--popular name for the moderate faction of the Hizb-i-Islami.

Khan--local landowner who supports local religious activities.

Mullah Omar--former head of the Taliban regime between 1995 and 2001

Naqashbandiyya --world Sufi order active especially in South and Southeast Asia.

National Liberation Front--secular movement supported by the Sunni establishment.

Quadariyya--second largest Sufi order in the world and especially active in Afghanistan.

Taliban--Radical fundamentalist group which ruled Afghanistan between 1995 and 2001 and sheltered Usama bin Laden until ousted by the American/NATO invasion.

Glossary for chapter on Azerbaijan

Albania--the ancient name for what is today Azerbaijan.

Aliyev--leader of Azerbaijan until his death in 2003

Ashura--Shia holiday commemorating the death of Hussein in 680 C.E

Azeri--an ethnic group divided between Iran (about 70% of the group) and an independent country (30%) in the southern Caucasus

Baku--capital of Azerbaijan.

Caucasus Mountains--area which separates Europe from Asia and which is the location for the republic of Azerbaijan.

Cyrillic Alphabet--The alphabet adopted and discarded by the Azeri in an attempt to forge links with Europe. It was replaced by Latin.

Eid--the final day of Ramadan or breaking the fast.

Islamic (ist) Party of Azerbaijan--Islamic party backed by Iran which has been outlawed,

Law of Freedom of Religion--law passed in the early 1990's that restored all religious property taken during the Soviet period.

Muharran--traditional holiday nominally Islamic which involves self-flagellation) which many Azeri consider their most important holiday in Islam.

Nagorno-Karabakh--area inhabited by Armenians/Azeri located outside the borders of Armenia which has now been occupied by Armenia.

Novroz--literally "new birth," this holiday which is a national holiday that dates before Islam, is celebrated on the vernal equinox, and is the most popular holiday in Azerbaijan.

Pan-Turkism--a movement whick seeks to unite all Turkic-speakers from Azerbaijan, Turkey, and Central Asia.

Salafists--a radical Islamic organization which originated from Egypt, and which is anti-Turkic and has been very active in missionary work and in the building of mosques.   Its activities are closely monitored by the government.

Shirk--a derogatory term loosely translated as anti-Islamic that refers to religion when expressed through nationalism as not following true religion.

Spiritual Board of the Transcaucasus--the supreme religious authority in the state with headquarters in Baku and with a Shia chair and Sunni vice-chair.

Glossary for chapter on Pakistan

Ahmadiya--a separate Muslim group which many Muslims do not consider mainstream Islamic

Baloch--one of the founding groups in Pakistan resident in Southwest Pakistan

Barelvi--pro-Sufi Sunni movement which opposes hardline Islamic extremism.

Bhutto--family which has been active in Pakistani politics for over two decades. It has given the country two prime ministers—the first, Ali Bhuttom was deposed and the second, Benazir Bhutto, was assassinated.

Chitor--one of the self-governing tribally-based (Pashtun) Northwest Provinces which are self-governimg.

Federal Shariat--The supreme interpreter of laws under Sharia in Pakistan..

Iqbal--Allama Muhammed Iqbal was one of the founders of the idea of a separate Muslim state to be formed out of India.

Islamabad--literally, the "abode of Islam," it was constructed in 1961 to be the capital of the country.

Islamic Assembly--a major political party in Pakistan.

Islamic Democratic Alliance--another major political party in Pakistan

Ismaili Sect--also called the Aga Khanis after its leader; it is an offshoot of the Shia branch of islam.

Jamiet-e-Ulema-Islam or JUI--a fundamentalist movement founded in the Pashtun/Pathan areas of the Northwest Provinces.

Jinnah--Muhammad al-Jinnah—founder and first leader of Pakistan.

Kashmiris--a founding ethnic group in Kashmir although Pakistan only occupies about one/third of the province. The occupation of much of the rest of Kashmir by India has been a source of conflict since 1947.

Lahore Resolution--the resolution passed by the Muslim League in 1940 which called for a separate Muslim state formed out of India.

Mirza--Iskander Mirza was an early leader of Pakistan.

Muhajir--Muslim immigrants from India who have emigrated to Pakistan.

Muslim League--venerable Islamic political party founded in 1906 in reaction to the partition of Bengal (1906-1911) which caused sectarian feeling.

Nazimiddun--Khaunja Nazimiddun was the chief aide to Jinnah.

Pakistani Intelligence Service (ISI)--Also known as the ISI, this service was an original backer of the Taliban and is still suspected of having some members who have radical Islamic leanings.

Punjabis--largest ethnic group in Pakistan and a relatively moderate force.

Purdah--term for seclusion of females under Islamic tradition

Pashtun--also known as Pathans, this group is located in the Northwest Provimces and is the most influenced by radical Islamic thinking,

Save Pakistan Movement--moderate Muslim movements which have combined resources against radical associations such as the Pakistani Taliban.

Sindhi--inhabitant of Sind in Southeast Pakistan which is the second most important province after Punjab.

Sunni United Council--an amalgam of moderate Sunni movements led by the Barelvi.

Waziristan--North and South Waziristan are the centers of Islamic extremist activity.

Zawahiri--Anwar Zawahiri is the successor of Usama bin Ladin and is believed to be hiding in Pakistan.

Zia--Muhammad Zia ul-Haq ruled from 1977 to 1988. During his rule, many measures which promoted Islam within the state were introduced.

Glossary for chapter on Bangladesh-
Awami League--one of two major political parties in contemporary Bangladesh.
Bangladesh Caliphate Movement--Bangladeshi movement which calls for a universal Islamic state.
Bangladesh Nationalist Party--the second major party in contemporary Bangladesh.
Bengal--A cultural geographical region which encompasses Hindu west Bengal now the Indian state of Bengal and east Muslim east Bengal now the nation of Bangladesh.
East Pakistan--the former name of Bangladesh when under Pakistan.
Fakir--itinerant holy man and spiritual guide.
Iman--person who conducts Islamic holy services at a mosque or madrassah.
Islamic United Front--orthodox Muslim group which opposed a close relationship between Bangladesh and Hindu India.
Maulvi--an iman who has had further education in religious studies.
Ministry of Religious Affairs-- a government organization which supports prayer, grounds, mosques, and pilgramages.
Mullah--local clerics who perform Islamic ceremonies such as weddings and funerals. They also often perform ceremonies based on pre-Islamic or non-Islamic traditions.
Muslim Family Ordinance--A law which covers areas such as inheritance, marriage, and divorce and incorporates Islamic traditions.
Partition of Bengal—the temporary (until 1911) partition between Hindu west Bengal and Muslim east Bengal (between 1905 and 1911) exacerbated communal feels and led to the formation of the Muslim League in order to protect Muslim rights.
Pirs-- similar to the fakirs but with a higher rank due to additional education.
Shab-e-Barat--This is the "festival of lights." It derives form a Hindu festival of lights and is an example of the degree of syncretism between Hindus and Muslims especially in the rural areas of Bangladesh.
Waqf--philanthropic religious foundations which exist in most Islamic countries, and is represented in Bangladesh by the Islamic National Foundation.
Younis--Muhammad Younis started a microcredit program that gave credit and small loans to poor people especially women usually in the countryside to start new businesses. Additional assistance was given in terms of free phones and other equipment. The program has been successful in rural Bangladesh.

Index

Bangladesh-